The Potato Book

By Myrna Davis

Foreword by Truman Capote

D1305641

William Morrow & Company, Inc., New York

First Morrow Quill Paperback Edition

Designed by Paul Davis

Library of Congress Catalog Card Number 73-7890

ISBN 0-688-05186-3

1 2 3 4 5 6 7 8 9 10

"What small potatoes we all are, compared to what we might be."

Charles Dudley Warner (1829-1900)

My Summer in a Garden

Introduction

The first edition of this book was published by the Hampton Day School in Bridgehampton, Long Island, as a fund-raising project for its scholarship fund. The school is a venture in open-classroom education and is situated on a former potato farm. Some of the classes are held in the old farmhouse, some in the newly renovated barn. The hundred or so students range from pre-kindergarten through high school, and many receive tuition aid. Potatoes seemed an appropriate subject for our efforts. Parents, teachers and friends submitted recipes. Special thanks are given to Janet Grossman and Deborah Perry for their diligent research, to Helen Rattray for her inspiration, to Irwin Glusker who began a book of his own on the same subject several years ago and provided us with much useful information, and finally to the artists who generously contributed their formidable talents.

Myrna Davis

Illustrations

Contents

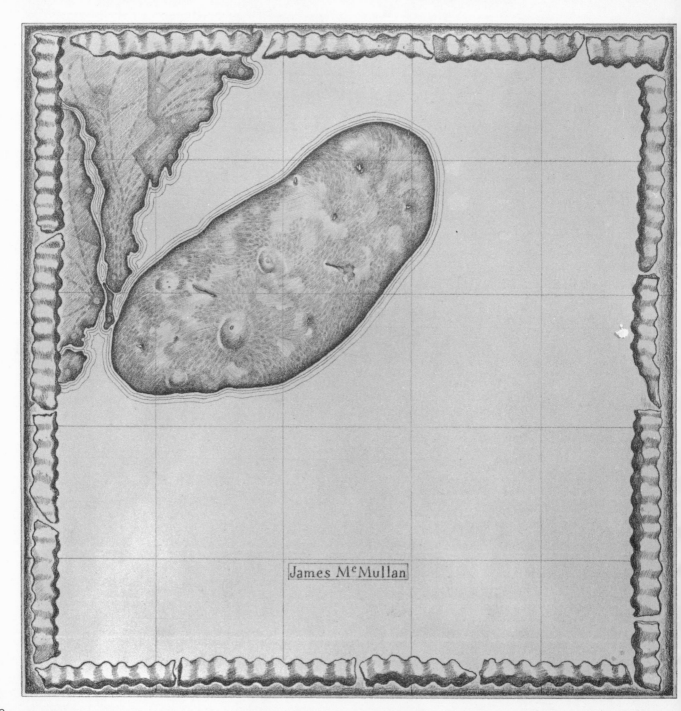

James McMullan

Foreword

I live in Sagaponack by the sea. The house, which I love, sits smack in the middle of potato fields. In Fall, when harvesting is done and the tractors are gone from the fields, I amble out through the empty rows collecting small, sweet, leftover potatoes for my larder.

Imagine a cold October morning. I fill my basket with found potatoes in the field and race to the kitchen to create my one and only most delicious ever potato lunch. The Russian vodka — it must be 80 proof — goes into the icebox to chill. The potatoes into the oven to bake. My breathless friend arrives to share the feast. Out comes the icy vodka. Out comes a bowl of sour cream. Likewise the potatoes, piping hot.

We sit down to sip our drinks. We split open steaming potatoes and put on some sour cream. *Now* I whisk out the big tin of caviar, which I have forgotten to tell you is the only way *I* can bear to eat a potato. Then caviar — the freshest, the grayest, the biggest Beluga — is heaped in mounds on the potato. My friend and I set to. This simple tribute to the fruit of Eastern Long Island farming makes an exhilarating country lunch, fuels the heart and soul and empties the pocketbook.

Some of the potato fields, so beautiful, flat and still, may not be here next year. And fewer the year after that. New houses are steadily popping up to mar the long line where the land ends and the sky begins.

The Hampton Day School is on a farm among these fields. It is as open in spirit as its surroundings and for that we can be thankful.

Truman Capote

The True History of the Potato by R.O. Blechman

Sir Pettibone Potato was a celebrated Botanist of 17th century England.

Among his discoveries were the Bananberry & the Liquid-Core Apple.

But during the reign of Oliver Cromwell the national taste changed.

Eager to change with the times, Sir Pettibone labored many years...

... to produce a Flat, Tasteless, Odorless Vegetable

However, the national taste had changed again.

Sir Pettibone Potato died a broken-hearted man, his vegetable ignored...

...until many years later, when plainer tastes prevailed.

A Grateful Nation erected a simple Granite Potato to mark his grave.

Potato Power

A Brief History of the Glorious Potato

The white, round or "Irish" potato, *Solanum tuberosum*, has graced the tables of peasants and of kings. It has been among the cheapest and most humble of vegetables, and also among the most dear, affordable only by gourmets of means. The potato has been slandered, stolen, and praised with monuments and legislation, its origins shrouded in conflicting legends for hundreds of years.

Credit for its discovery and importation to Europe was given to Sir Walter Raleigh in 1693, when it was believed that he had brought it back from America over one hundred years earlier. That was later proved impossible, for while the Indians cultivated certain other tubers, the *Solanum tuberosum* did not arrive in America until the eighteenth century. Sir Francis Drake was honored for the same contribution with a statue in Baden, Germany, but the potato had reached Europe before his time by a different route.

"Pray for peace and grace and spiritual food, For Wisdom and guidance, for all these are good, But don't forget the potatoes."

John Tyler Pettee (1822-1907) *Prayer and Potatoes*

The potato's original habitat was Peru, and it was the Spanish *conquistadors* who discovered it in the mountains of Chile and Ecuador during their adventures in South America during the mid-sixteenth century. The date of its first appearance in Europe is not exact, but potatoes are known to have been washed up on the Irish coast from wrecks of the Spanish Armada returning from Peru in 1565. In Peru itself, the potato goes back to prehistoric times, representations of which have been found in unearthed tombs.

The name "potato" is an English corruption of *batata*, the West Indian name for sweet potato, the latter not being related botanically to *Solanum tuberosum* at all. But reports of this and other edible tubers around the world during the sixteenth and seventeenth centuries led to confusion and helped to obscure the potato's true origins.

The Spaniards called the potato *papa*, its native Peruvian name meaning "tuber," although some of the *conquistadors* described it as *turma de tierra*, the name for truffle which means, literally, "earth testicle." While it is hard to imagine a comparison between the delicate truffle and the sturdy potato, the likening persisted in various languages and remains a synonym, for example, in Germany, where the potato is called both *Kartoffel*, a modification of *Tartuffel* or truffle, and *Erdapfel*, or "earth apple." The latter is related to the French *pomme de terre*, of course, or "apple of the earth." *Kartofel* survives as the potato's appellative link with the truffle in Russia and Poland. In Italy, the early name for potato was *tartuffo* and the truffle was *tartufi*; today *patate* is used. In Spain today, *papa* and *patata* are synomymous.

At first, the potato was considered no more than a botanical curiosity in Europe. It is, along with the tomato and eggplant, a member of the large, and largely infamous, Nightshade family of plants, noted for their poisonous and narcotic properties. No other edible plant in Europe at that time was grown from anything but seed, and so the unusual habits and appearance of the potato aroused suspicions of evil.

The bulbous, irregular nodules suggested deformity, and superstitious opinion blamed the potato for leprosy, scrofula, syphilis and various other illnesses and disease. Indeed, as late as the eighteenth century in Russia, peasants died of famine rather than cultivate the potato which they believed to be un-Christian and sexually unclean because it reproduced by budding rather than by sexual fertilization. The hapless vegetable was accused of hermaphroditism and masturbation, even being formally tried and burned at stake on occasion.

When the potato did begin to attain acceptance as a food, superstitions lingered, such as instructions that they be planted only under a full moon, or early in the morning. Even today in Ireland and other countries, potato-planting often is synchronized with Good Friday, and other Christian and magic rituals are called upon to assist the growth and harvest.

Ireland was one of the first European countries to cultivate the potato on a large scale. Their climate was so suitable that potatos eventually replaced almost all other crops. They were eaten for breakfast, lunch and dinner, and used as a source for a whiskey called *poteen*, named after the small pots used for making it. The Irish loved the vegetable, calling it by such pet names as "Flowery" or "Laughing Potato." Its very success and the dependence it caused led to the deaths of an estimated 600,000 people during the terrible famine of 1846 when a blight destroyed the year's entire crop.

The potato was recorded in England in 1585, in Italy at the same time, and in 1588 in Austria. The monarchs of Prussia were eager to propagate the potato, and in 1651 Frederick William I threatened to cut off the noses and ears of all those who refused to plant them. Frederick's son, Frederick II, gave away seed potatoes and forced the peasants to cultivate them, backing up his edict with threats from his dragoons.

In France, the potato was attacked by physicians who believed it was a dangerous aphrodisiac and responsible for many maladies, only the least of which was indigestion. Agronomists contended that it would ruin any soil in which it was planted. But the potato had a champion in Antoine Auguste Parmentier, a French pharmacist who had developed an enthusiasm for eating potatoes during his imprisonment in Germany during the Seven Years War. Determined to popularize the tuber in his own country, he gave a formal dinner for Benjamin Franklin, Lavoisier and other prominent persons, which consisted entirely of potatoes prepared in various ways. He also persuaded Louis XVI to give him permission to plant potatoes in a sandy field outside of Paris, "Les Sablons," noted for its barrenness. The plants flourished, and Parmentier arranged to have the fields guarded by uniformed soldiers during the day to arouse the interest of local farmers. Each night the soldiers withdrew and the unprotected potatoes were stolen by the covetous populace, either to be eaten or planted. When the field was in full bloom, Parmentier presented a bouquet of potato blossoms to the King. Marie Antoinette wore one in her hair, and the King replied, "France will thank you some day for having found bread for the poor." Today most potato dishes in France still are termed *a la parmentier*, and potato blossoms bloom each year on Parmentier's grave.

Potatoes were slow to achieve popularity in England and Scotland until the mid-eighteenth century, perhaps partly attributable to the poor quality of the tubers. Improved varieties were developed with selective breeding, finally establishing potatoes as a staple crop.

The potato came to North America in 1719. It was planted in Londonderry, New Hampshire, by Scotch-Irish immigrants, and from there spread around the country. One of the regions in which it found a natural home was the eastern end of Long Island, where the soil consists of a mixture of silt, clay and sand, porous and moderately acid, designated "Bridgehampton loam," by the United States Department of Agriculture, and unique in the United States. Bridgehampton loam is found in an area of about 50 miles square, bounded by Southampton to the west, Amagansett to the east, the Atlantic Ocean to the south and Peconic Bay and Gardiner's Island to the north. In it are grown the famous Long Island potatoes, of which there are several varieties. Green Mountains are a favorite in the area, believed to be as suitable for baking as for boiling by its proponents, but many others such as Katahdins and Russet Burbanks also fare well.

Long Island growers buy seed potatoes for each new planting, rather than using their own potatoes for this purpose. Seed potatoes are immature potatoes generally grown in Maine, upstate New York or Canada, where the frost kills the vine before the potatoes, and therefore any diseases, have a chance to fully develop. The farmers plant sections of the seed potatoes which contain the eyes, and these may produce up to twenty times their own weight in eating potatoes. Actual potato seeds come from the blossoms, but these seldom reproduce true to type and are of interest only to breeders trying to develop new varieties.

One acre of land can produce up to six hundred bushels of potatoes, although half that amount is closer to average. Since potatoes require no milling to be edible, as do grains, they are unequaled as a food crop for food value and economy.

The growing season on Long Island is from mid-April until early September. After harvesting, the fields generally are planted with rye which is plowed under in the spring. Once the potatoes are dug up, they are stored in huge barns built half under ground. This picturesque kind of construction helps maintain the desirable temperature and humidity, as the greatest dangers to potatoes come from dryness, sunlight, frost and heat.

Sometimes it is difficult to find Long Island potatoes in Long Island markets, as they are trucked up and down the coast from Canada to Florida and as far west as the Mississippi. But even when they are abundantly available locally, it is not an uncommon sight to see well-dressed passers-by stopping their cars at the roadside to gather the tiny new potatoes the reapers have left behind. These precious nuggets, it is claimed, are unparalleled in sweetness, a judgement not unprejudiced, surely, by the stolen joy of taking one's sustenance directly from the earth.

Potato Primer

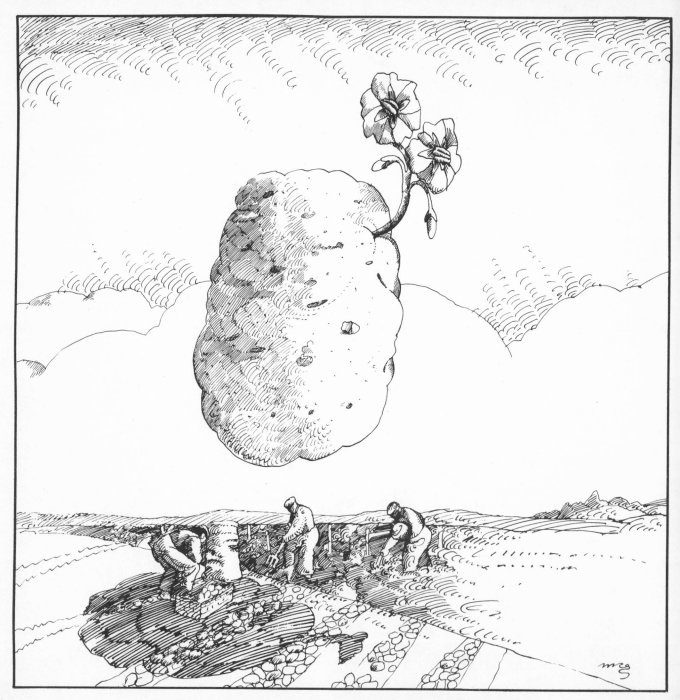

How to Buy Potatoes

There are a great many varieties of potatoes grown in the United States, including Chippewa, Cobbler, Green Mountain, Katahdin, Kennebec, Ontario, Pontiac, Russet Burbank and Sebago, to mention some of the more usual, but they are rarely marketed under these names. Most potatoes are labeled simply "all-purpose" or "baking."

Baking potatoes are mealy in texture, and light and fluffy when baked properly, but fall apart easily in other types of preparation. The most popular in the United States is the Russet Burbank from Idaho. Late-season Katahdin, Maine and Long Island Russet are generally good for this purpose, too. Firm, smooth potatoes with a regular shape and attractive appearance give best results.

The all-purpose potato, such as Long Island's Katahdin, is somewhat waxier in texture and holds its shape better in boiling, creaming and salad-making. Irregular shapes or surface dents do not affect the taste and often cost less per pound, but may increase waste and peeling time.

Potatoes with green sunburn spots, worm damage or rot should be avoided.

"New" or early potatoes are thin-skinned, tender and cook quickly. They are best prepared with the skins left on. Buy only enough to use for a week or ten days, as they do not store well.

"Old" or mature potatoes, those that have been stored and are available in the winter, are particularly good for pancakes, dumplings and salads with dressing because they have lost moisture and are more absorbent.

Potatoes may be sold graded or ungraded according to U.S. standards, unless packaged in closed containers in which case they must be either graded or labeled "unclassified." Grades indicate size, shape, defects, etc. and not nutritive or cooking quality. *U.S. Fancy* are the highest grade, and premium-priced for uniformity. *U.S. No. 1* is the grade generally available to consumers, with varying size but none smaller than 1-7/8 inches in diameter. *U.S. Commercial* is sold to large-quantity buyers, *U.S. No. 2* is sold for feed, starch and other manufacturing purposes.

How to Store Potatoes

Potatoes should be stored in a cool, dark, dry place. For short-term storage of two to three weeks, a temperature between 50 degrees and 70 degrees Fahrenheit is recommended. For longer periods, potatoes should be stored at about 45 degrees.

Potatoes should not be stored in the refrigerator, or where the temperature is likely to fall below 40 degrees, because cold will cause the potato starch to convert to sugars and produce an undesirably sweet taste when cooked. Should this occur, however, allow potatoes to stand for several days at room temperature to convert the sugars back to starch.

Exposure to light should be avoided. A few days of exposure can turn the potato's surface green, and these discolored areas may be bitter or even toxic.

New potatoes will not keep well for more than one or two weeks at the most.

Sprouts which may appear can be picked off, and sprouted potatoes are still usable even if soft.

FREEZING Raw potatoes get soft when frozen. Cooked potatoes become mushy and grainy if frozen in liquid, so it is best to omit them from stews, casseroles or other dishes planned for freezing.

Mashed and stuffed potatoes freeze well. When mashing, do so thoroughly to keep air out of mixture. Add one tablespoon of butter for each pound of potatoes, and enough milk to achieve desired consistency, and season to taste.

French-fried potatoes and fried potato puffs also freeze well, and will retain their quality for about two months at zero degrees Fahrenheit. Reheat in 350 degree oven spread out on a cookie sheet.

How to Prepare Potatoes

The four basic ways of preparing potatoes are boiling, steaming, baking and frying, either peeled or unpeeled. After this first cooking, they may be served plain, or used as the basis for mashed potatoes, salads and other more elaborate recipes.

BOILING UNPEELED This method preserves the full nutritive value and flavor. Scrub the jackets gently with a vegetable brush to remove any dirt. Place potatoes in cold water with 2 or 3 teaspoons of salt per quart, and bring to a boil. Cook for 25 to 40 minutes uncovered until tender. Then drain off water, cover with a clean folded cloth, and shake pan over low heat to allow potatoes to dry on all sides.

BOILING PEELED Pare potatoes with a potato-peeler or small paring knife. Remove and discard sprouts, eyes and any discolored portions. Allow peeled potatoes to sit in lightly-salted water for one-half to two hours, and use this water for cooking to preserve nutrients. For cooking, allow one-half teaspoon of salt for each quart of water. Put potatoes back in the cold salted water and bring to a boil. Cook steadily for 20 to 40 minutes, uncovered, until tender. Drain, and cover with a clean dry cloth to absorb the steam. If the potatoes begin to disintegrate during cooking, as sometimes happens with old potatoes, drain immediately, cover with a clean cloth and allow them to finish cooking over low heat.

Save the parings. These can be boiled later and the liquid strained for use in soups and sauces, retaining flavor and vitamins.

NOTES ON BOILING If the potatoes are quartered instead of whole, cooking time will be 20 to 25 minutes.
To keep potatoes white, add a teaspoon of vinegar or lemon juice to the soaking water. They will keep 3 or 4 days in the refrigerator this way.
A little milk in the cooking water will also keep potatoes white and improve their flavor.
A dash of sugar instead of salt with boiling potatoes adds flavor and helps to retain the Vitamin C.

STEAMING Place scrubbed or pared potatoes into one-quarter cup of boiling water, cover tightly and cook 12 to 20 minutes or until tender. If the pot does not distribute the steam uniformly, steam the potatoes on a rack, or in a steaming basket or strainer above the water, covered by a lid or heavy plate.

BAKING UNPEELED This is just about the simplest method of preparing potatoes. *Any* potato can be baked, but for the desired flaky texture it is recommended that mature, baking-type potatoes such as the Russet be used. The higher the oven temperature, the shorter the cooking time will be and the crustier the skin.

At 350 degrees Fahrenheit, a medium-size potato will take about an hour and a quarter to bake. At 400 degrees it will take about one hour, and at 450 degrees just 45 minutes.

For a soft skin, rub the potato with olive oil, butter or other shortening.

For a crisp, crusty skin, line the oven floor with aluminum foil, preheat to 250 or 300 degrees, place the potatoes on the foil and bake slowly until tender, turning halfway through cooking.

In either case, be sure to pierce the skin with a fork to allow steam to escape, or the potato may explode during baking.

Plain yogurt mixed with fresh or frozen chopped chives or mint makes a delicious low-calorie topping for baked potatoes.

Wrapping the potato in aluminum foil will produce a soft skin, too, but technically this is steaming rather than baking as the moisture in the potato remains trapped, and the light flaky texture will be missing.

For outdoor barbecue-baked potatoes, wrap scrubbed, dried potatoes in foil and prick through the foil and potatoes. Place on a grill or in the coals, turning occasionally, until tender.

SHORTCUT Parboil potatoes for about five minutes, drain and dry, and then bake. This will reduce the baking time by half.

BAKING PEELED Coat potatoes with butter, olive oil or other shortening and place in a shallow baking dish or pan. Bake at above temperatures, allowing an extra one-half to two hours, depending upon size.

NOTES ON BAKING A muffin tin makes a convenient container for baking several potatoes at once. A baking nail or long, clean nail through the center of each potato will speed up the baking time and add some lightness to the texture. Leftover baked potatoes can be refrigerated for later use in frying, stuffing, etcetera.

FRYING RAW POTATOES IN SHALLOW FAT

Shred or slice peeled or scrubbed unpeeled potatoes. Heat one-quarter inch of melted butter or shortening in a heavy skillet, add potatoes and cook, covered, over low heat for 15 minutes. When potatoes are tender, uncover, increase heat, and cook about 10 minutes more or until brown. Dust lightly with paprika for faster browning.

FRYING COOKED POTATOES IN SHALLOW FAT

Slice or dice cooked potatoes, peeled or unpeeled, and fry as above, uncovered. Turn with spatula to brown both sides. These are known variously as "cottage fries," "home fries," or "hash browned" potatoes. Mashed potatoes may be fried in the same manner.

Finely ground bread crumbs may be added for texture towards the end of the cooking.

Cream and grated or sauteed onions may be added also to enrich the texture.

Boiling oil can be kept from splattering in a fondue pot by placing a large slice of raw potato in the oil.

FRYING IN DEEP FAT

Peel the potatoes and cut into strips, chips, shreds, balls or other desired shape using a sharp knife, fluted vegetable slicer or ball scoop. Soak softened potatoes in ice water for about one-half hour to firm them. Cold storage potatoes should be soaked for about 15 minutes in cool water, about 90 degrees, to insure a nice light color when fried, and then dried with a towel to remove excess starch and moisture. Using a deep heavy kettle or saucepan, or an electric fryer if you have one, fill about one-third full with a vegetable oil such as peanut, corn, safflower or sesame oil, or an equivalent amount of solid all-purpose shortening, and heat slowly to 300 to 330 degrees. Drop in the potatoes, a handful at a time, and allow them to cook for about two minutes or until sputtering stops. Using a slotted spoon, remove potatoes and drain on paper towels or brown paper for five minutes. Raise heat of cooking oil to 375 degrees. Put drained potatoes into a wire frying basket, and slowly lower them into the hot oil. Fry for about three minutes, remove and drain on paper. Serve immediately, uncovered.

NOTES ON FRYING

Mature baking potatoes are recommended for successful French fries, souffle potatoes and potato chips.

FRENCH FRIES

Slice potatoes into strips two and one-half inches long and about one-quarter to one-half inch in width.

POTATO CHIPS

Slice potatoes as thin as possible with a potato peeler, and soak in ice water for two hours, changing the water each hour. Drain and dry thoroughly. Heat oil slowly to 380 degrees. Separate the raw chips, place in a wire frying basket and drop into hot fat, shaking frequently to keep the chips from sticking to each other.

MASHED POTATOES Boil, bake or steam the potatoes. Peel and mash with a potato masher, fork or whisk, or put into a food mill or electric blender. Add about one tablespoon of butter, one-third cup hot milk or cream and one-half teaspoon salt per potato, and beat until fluffy and light. Serve at once if possible. Egg yolks may be added for richness and taste about one for every two potatoes. (These are known as *Duchesse* potatoes.)

TO KEEP MASHED POTATOES WARM Put mashed potatoes in the top of a double boiler, or place the bowl or pot of potatoes in a pan of hot water in a slow oven.

Mashed turnips will be less thin if a potato is mashed into the mixture.

To thicken soups, grate three tablespoons of raw potato for each cup of soup and simmer until the potato is absorbed, about 15 minutes.

Recipes

Hors d'Oeuvres

Pigs In Blankets

1 pound sausage links cut into quarters
1 egg
2 cups mashed potatoes
Salt and pepper
Flour
2 tablespoons sausage drippings

Saute sausage pieces until cooked and drain on paper towels. Beat egg, add potatoes, salt and pepper to taste, and mix thoroughly. Place a spoonful of the potato mixture on a lightly-floured board and a sausage piece on top of it. Roll gently so that the sausage is wrapped in the potato. Chill until ready to brown.

Shortly before serving, heat sausage drippings in skillet or chafing dish and brown the rolls until slightly crisp. Serve with toothpicks and mustard or mustard-relish dip.

Matchsticks

1 pound potatoes
Cooking oil
Salt or garlic salt

Peel potatoes and wash well. Cut into thinnest possible slivers and soak in ice water for half an hour. Drain and dry, and immerse in boiling oil for one to one-and-a-half minutes. Drain on paper towels, immerse a second time and drain again. Sprinkle with salt or garlic salt, and serve hot or at room temperature. These are good with cocktails.

Potato Mysteries

4 cups mashed potatoes
2 eggs
¼ cup cracker meal or matzo meal
1½ teaspoons salt
½ teaspoon freshly ground black pepper
¾ cup ground cooked beef, chicken or liver
2 teaspoons grated onion
2 tablespoons melted shortening
Cooking oil for deep frying

Beat eggs. Mix in the potatoes, cracker meal, one-half teaspoon of salt and one-quarter teaspoon of pepper until smooth. Divide into 12 pieces and flatten each on a lightly-floured board. Mix beef, chicken or liver with onion, shortening and remaining seasoning, and place one teaspoon of this mixture on each piece of dough. Pinch the edges of the dough together to form a dumpling, and drop into 370 degree oil until browned. Drain and serve with toothpicks.

Soups

Vichyssoise

This soup, although a version of the French *potage Parmentier*, a leek and potato soup, is actually an American invention.

4 tablespoons butter
3 large leeks
1 small yellow onion
1 small stalk celery
6 medium-size potatoes
4 cups chicken stock, preferably fresh
Salt
White pepper
1 cup heavy cream
4 teaspoons chopped chives

Peel the potatoes and slice about one-quarter inch thick. Peel, wash and finely chop the white part of the leeks, and the onion. Melt the butter in a saucepan and saute the leeks and onion slowly until lightly golden and translucent, add the stock and potatoes and bring to a boil. Reduce the heat, cover partially, and cook for 40 minutes or until the potatoes crumble easily when pierced. Then, using a food mill or sieve, puree the mixture into a large bowl. Add salt and pepper to taste, and chill. When cold, add the heavy cream and more seasoning if necessary. Pour into chilled bowls and top with chives. Serves 6 to 8.

VARIATION

WATERCRESS SOUP Add one packed cup of thoroughly washed watercress leaves to the mixture for the last five minutes of cooking, and puree as above. Garnish with blanched watercress leaves instead of chives.

New England Clam Chowder

⅛ pound lean salt pork, chopped fine
1 large yellow onion, quartered and sliced fine
3 small stalks celery
¼ cup butter
1 pint large chowder clams (quahogs), chopped,
  and their liquid
1 cup potatoes, peeled and cubed
1 quart milk (cream may be substituted for part of
  the milk for a richer chowder)
1 tablespoon chopped fresh parsley
½ teaspoon paprika
1 tablespoon flour

Fry chopped salt pork over low heat until crisp, remove from pan and drain on absorbent paper. Drain off excess fat from pan. Add butter, saute onion and celery until transparent. Add flour, stir and cook for another minute, then remove from heat.

Chop clams, saving the clam juice. Wash thoroughly in water to remove all the sand, and strain water and clam juice through layers of cheesecloth into a bowl to remove sand. Add to a saucepan with the potatoes and simmer until potatoes are tender. Add sauteed onion and celery, and chop the clams well and add, too. Simmer for a few minutes without boiling. Meanwhile, scald the milk and then add to the vegetables and clams. Sprinkle with paprika, chopped parsley and crumbled pork before serving. Makes about one and one-half quarts.

Manhattan Clam Chowder

Polly and Ed Kovaleski, Sag Harbor

¼ pound bacon or salt pork
½ cup chopped onions
1 quart clams chopped and their liquid
1 stalk celery, diced
2 small carrots, diced
1 quart water
1 large can tomatoes
¼ cup catsup
4 potatoes, peeled and diced
½ teaspoon oregano

Fry bacon or salt pork in a deep pot. Drain off excess fat and saute onions in remainder. Wash clams well in a bowl of water, and strain this water and the clam juice through several layers of cheescloth to remove all sand. Chop clams and add clams, clam juice, water, tomatoes, catsup, potatoes and oregano to bacon and onions and simmer over low heat for two to three hours. Even better the next day.

Quahog Chowder For 100

Helen and Everett Rattray, Amagansett, N.Y.

1 bushel chowder (Quahog) clams, opened and minced
15 pounds dressed-weight striped bass fillets, chunked
1¾ gallons clam broth reserved from steaming open clams (plus 1 quart)
18 medium-size onions minced fine and squeezed
2 pounds salt pork, diced
½ pound butter
10 pounds potatoes, pared and diced
3 quarts milk
1 cup Almaden white wine
Thyme, one bunch minced
1 cup chopped fresh parsley

Try out pork, add onion and cook until just slightly brown. Add butter if necessary. Add clam broth. Bring to boil. Add potatoes; cook until tender. Add fish; cook until half or three-quarters done. Add clams, simmer briefly. Add thyme and parsley. Add milk and wine. Simmer all a while.

Potato And Salmon Chowder

4 cups peeled, cubed potatoes
1 cup sliced carrots
1 tablespoon salt
3 cups water
1 package frozen peas
⅓ cup butter
⅓ cup chopped onion
¼ cup flour
5 cups milk
1 pound can salmon, flaked (with skin and bones removed)
1 cup thinly sliced celery
½ teaspoon Worcestershire sauce

Put potatoes, carrots, water and salt into a saucepan, bring to a boil, lower heat and simmer until tender, about 15 minutes. Add frozen peas, bring to a boil, and remove from heat at once.

Saute onion in melted butter in a skillet until golden, add flour and stir until smooth. Cook for one minute, add two and one-half cups milk and stir constantly over low flame until the mixture gets thick. Add salmon and salmon liquid to the vegetables. Add white sauce, celery, Worcestershire sauce and the remaining milk. Reheat before serving. Serves 12.

Potato And Oyster Stew

2 cups peeled and diced potatoes
1 cup water
2 teaspoons salt
1 pint oysters, drained and chopped
1 pint oyster liquor or oyster liquor and milk
⅓ cup butter
1 cup light cream
⅛ teaspoon white pepper
¼ teaspoon paprika

Put potatoes and salt into a saucepan with the water and boil 10 minutes. Add oysters and oyster liquor and heat to boiling point. Remove from heat before boiling, stir in butter, light cream, pepper and paprika. Cover and allow to cool at room temperature for 15 minutes. Serves six.

Caraway Potato Soup

This recipe was given to me by Mr. Famenik who has sold architectural books in New York for many years. My husband and I are both architects who love to cook.
Belva Shaw, Sagaponack

Cook three mature potatoes, peeled and cubed, in a large pot with six to eight cups of salted water and one-half teaspoon of caraway seeds. Thicken slightly with flour if necessary. Add one-half pint of prepared sour cream and serve.

Mashed Potato Soup

2 cups leftover mashed potatoes
1 cup chopped onion
4 tablespoons butter
1 quart milk
Salt and pepper
Chopped parsley or chives

Melt butter in saucepan. Chop onion and saute until lightly colored and transparent. Add mashed potatoes and mix well. Blend in milk and seasoning and heat to boiling point, stirring constantly. Remove from heat at once. Garnish with chopped parsley or chives and serve.

VARIATION For a complete meal, slice a few frankfurters into thin rounds, saute lightly and mix into soup. Serve with a hearty green salad such as watercress.

Potatomato Soup

In thickening soups and sauces with potato flour, keep in mind that one teaspoon is the equivalent of one tablespoon of regular flour.

5 cups water
4 to 5 tablespoons fresh chopped basil tied in
  cheesecloth (or 2 heaping teaspoons dried basil)
3 cups finely chopped onions
1 green pepper, finely chopped
3 tablespoons vegetable oil
4 cups peeled tomatoes, fresh or canned
1 teaspoon sugar
2 teaspoons salt
½ teaspoon paprika
3 tablespoons butter
3 tablespoons flour
2 cups hot milk
2 cups boiled potatoes, peeled and cubed

Put water in large kettle with a bag of basil, cover and bring to a boil. Lower heat and simmer for about a half-hour. Remove bag and reserve liquid. Heat oil in a large skillet and saute onions and pepper until tender. Add tomatoes, sugar, salt and paprika. Melt butter in another saucepan, add flour and blend in well, then add the milk, stirring constantly until smooth. Pour this cream sauce into the skillet with the vegetables. Continue to stir, add potatoes and basil liquid, and cook until hot but not boiling. Serves eight.

COLD Prepare as above, omitting cream sauce. Pour tomato mixture into blender and puree, then return to saucepan. Put potatoes into blender with two cups cold milk and puree. Add to tomato mixture with basil liquid and heat to boiling point. Allow to cool slightly, then chill in refrigerator until ready to serve.

Salads

Basic Potato Salad

6 medium potatoes, boiled, pared and diced
 (about 5 cups)
½ cup diced celery
2 tablespoons finely chopped parsley
2 teaspoons chopped onion (optional)
1 cup mayonnaise
¼ cup vinegar
1 teaspoon salt
Paprika
Pepper

Combine potatoes, celery, parsley and onion.
Blend mayonnaise, vinegar, salt and paprika and
pepper to taste. Mix all together, cover and chill.
Serves six.

VARIATIONS

EGG AND BACON Add four hard-boiled eggs,
chopped, and eight cooked, crumbled bacon
strips before mixing.

BEAN Add two whole scallions, chopped, one-
quarter cup thinly sliced black olives, one cup
canned kidney or lima beans, drained, one-quarter
teaspoon oregano, one firm cucumber, peeled and
diced, and three hard-boiled eggs, sliced.

SHRIMP Add chopped shrimp. Chopped chives
may be substituted for the onion.

NUTS Add one cup chopped Brazil nuts.

Sour Cream Potato Salad

Judith Hope, East Hampton

4 cups boiled, peeled and diced potatoes
1 cup diced cucumber
3 tablespoons minced onion
1½ teaspoons salt
½ teaspoon pepper
3 hard-boiled eggs, diced

Mix the above and toss with the following
 dressing:
1½ cups sour cream
½ cup mayonnaise
¼ cup red wine vinegar
¾ teaspoon celery seed
1 teaspoon prepared mustard

Chill until ready to serve. For six.

Red On Red Potato Salad

Peel and slice large boiled potatoes. Combine red vinegar from a can of pickled beets with an equal amount of Worcestershire sauce and a dash of onion juice. Marinate potatoes in liquid, top with beets and refrigerate. Toss before serving.

Green On Green Potato Salad

12 medium potatoes
½ cup chopped parsley
½ cup chopped green pepper
½ cup chopped celery tops
¼ cup chopped scallions
¼ cup chopped dill pickle
1 cup mayonnaise
¼ cup French dressing (oil and vinegar)
2 teaspoons salt
½ teaspoon freshly ground pepper
1 teaspoon dry mustard

Boil potatoes, then cool, peel and dice coarsely. Mix all the green ingredients together, set aside about one-half cup, and toss the remainder with the potatoes, mayonnaise, French dressing and seasonings. Transfer to a serving bowl, and top with the reserved greens. Chill. Serves eight to ten.

Hot Or Cold Mashed Potato Salad

4 cups hot mashed potatoes
⅓ cup mayonnaise
1 tablespoon vinegar
1 teaspoon salt
1½ tablespoons chopped green pepper
1½ tablespoons finely chopped pimiento
¾ cup finely chopped celery
¾ cup finely chopped onion
2 or 3 hard-cooked eggs, chopped (optional)

Mix well and heat or chill. Serves six.

VARIATIONS

HOT Crisp bacon bits and chopped parsley may be substituted for the green pepper and pimiento.

COLD Six to eight finely chopped gherkins and one small can of tiny peas may be substituted for the green pepper.

Mushroom Potato Salad

Peel and slice cold boiled potatoes in a bowl. Drop a little olive oil on each slice and let stand until absorbed. Mince and stew fresh mushrooms in enough water to cover, then pour mushrooms and liquid over the potatoes and chill before serving.

Salade Nicoise

This is especially good for beach picnics and summer luncheons. It can be prepared well ahead of time and chilled until ready to serve.

Miriam Mednick, Philadelphia

8 potatoes, cooked, peeled and sliced
4 eggs, hard-boiled and sliced
1 can tuna
1 can anchovies
½ cup capers
½ cup black olives
1 pimiento, sliced
2 tomatoes, diced
2 onions, sliced
Vinegar, olive oil, salt, pepper to taste
Watercress

In a large serving bowl, put a layer of sliced potatoes, a layer of eggs, tuna, anchovies, olives, tomatoes and onions. Season with vinegar, olive oil, salt and pepper and repeat layers until finished. Decorate with pimiento and watercress.

New Potato Salad

Cold leftover new potatoes which have been boiled in their jackets make a delicious salad. Slice each potato in half, marinate in oil and vinegar dressing with salt and freshly ground pepper to taste, and any or all the following ingredients: Capers, crisp bacon bits, leftover cooked green beans or peas, chopped anchovies, chopped cooked or raw carrots. Chill before serving.

Boiled Potato Dishes

Raclette

We discovered this apres-ski dish in Switzerland, where each helping is served on a separate plate. The used plates are stacked at the table as they are emptied, and it is not uncommon to see 18 to 20 plates piled up in front of a diner at the end of a meal.

Cecile Schacht, Pelham. N.Y.

Fontina cheese
New potatoes boiled in their jackets
Cocktail onions
Gherkins

Traditionally, this dish is prepared over a wood or charcoal fire, and derives its name from the French verb *racler*, "to scrape." Hold the cut side of the cheese against the fire, turning frequently to prevent dripping. When it begins to get bubbly, scrape with a knife onto a heated plate, and serve with a boiled new potato. Bowls of cocktail onions and gherkins should be offered on the side as an accompaniment. The cheese may also be prepared by slicing thinly and placed under a broiler on a cookie sheet to melt. The cheese should hold its shape and get bubbly and crisp.

There is a Swiss cheese called Raclette which is used for this dish, and also Bagnes cheese, but these are less generally available.

Cottage Supper

The Irish generally cooked their potatoes one way, by boiling, and always with the skins on. There was a time in England, however, when an unpeeled potato was described as *en robe de chambre,* or "in its dressing gown," and was acceptable only on informal occasions.

2 pounds new potatoes
8 ounces cottage cheese
½ pint sour cream
1 bunch scallions
1 ounce caraway seeds
Salt

Boil potatoes in their skins in salted water. Serve hot with separate bowls of sour cream, chopped scallions and caraway seeds as accompaniment.

New Potato Fondue

2 pounds new potatoes, extra small
½ cup butter or olive oil
½ cup wine vinegar
¼ cup minced onion
1 teaspoon oregano
Salt
Dash of cayenne pepper

Boil potatoes in their jackets, drain and dry. Put butter or oil in fondue pot, along with the vinegar, onion, oregano and seasonings. Heat but do not boil. Keeping the heat steady at this point, serve bowls of the tiny new potatoes along with fondue forks and napkins. This makes a good buffet dish or as a first course for a small-table dinner.

Baked Potato Dishes

Baked Potatoes In Crust Shells

Kay Zachary, Amagansett

Bake large Long Island Russet or Idaho potatoes until thoroughly done. Cut in half and remove potato with a teaspoon dipped in butter so that the potato pieces do not fall apart. Butter empty shell and place under broiler. When crusty, mound potato pieces inside shells. Sprinkle with finely chopped parsley and serve.

Millionaire's Baked Potatoes

Herb McCarthy's, Southampton

6 large baking potatoes
Cream
1 tablespoon onion, grated
¼ teaspoon monosodium glutamate
Salt to taste
Caviar

Scrub potatoes well and bake. Cut off tops and scoop out cooked potato and mash. Add onions and seasonings and beat well. Heap seasoned potato into shells and at serving time, heat in a 400 degree oven for 15 minutes. Top each potato with caviar.

Fancy Baked Potatoes

There is not much excuse for going to the trouble of this recipe — plain baked potatoes being so easy and so satisfactory — except that these spuds are (a) different, (b) eliminate the hassle of putting on butter or sour cream or whatever at the table, (c) are inclined to be a lot more decorative around a piece of meat or fish or fowl, and (d) will keep fairly well in a warm oven for an hour or so after they are done.

John Shinn, East Hampton

Any kind of potatoes will do, provided they are peeled and cut into a long narrow shape — ideally, about two inches thick by three-and-a-half inches long. Cut a slice of the bottom of each potato so that it sits squarely and firmly on a chopping board. Using a very sharp knife, cut each potato into one-eighth-inch slices, being very careful not to cut through to the bottom. Then roll each potato thoroughly in a pan containing one stick of melted butter.

Place potatoes in a baking pan and sprinkle the top of each with coarse (kosher) salt, freshly ground or cracked black pepper, and as much paprika as you think is pretty. Bake for one hour in a 375 degree oven, basting two or three times with the melted butter that will collect in the pan.

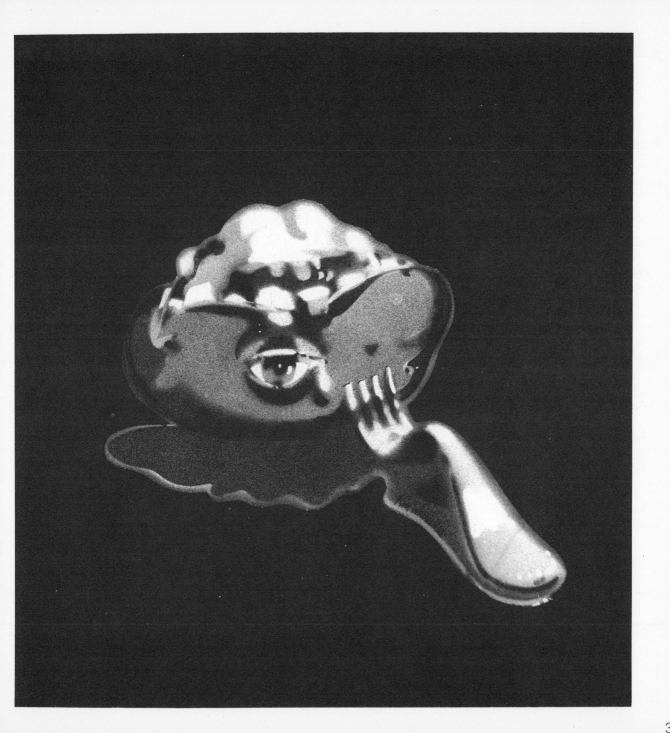

Savonette Potatoes

The French at time give whimsical names to their dishes and one of my favorite recipes is called in French, *pommes savonettes* or "small soap bar potatoes." The name derives from the shape of the potatoes in which they are cut and trimmed to look like small bars of soap. This is an incredibly simple recipe to make.

Craig Claiborne, East Hampton

1½ to 2 pounds large potatoes (about three)
Salt to taste
2 tablespoons butter
1 tablespoon peanut, vegetable or corn oil

Preheat oven to 425 degrees. Peel the potatoes and trim the ends to make them flat. Cut the potatoes into slices about one inch thick or less. Trim the edges slightly to make the slices look like soap bars. Rinse the potato slices in cold water and drain. Arrange the potato slices in one layer in a fairly wide, heat-proof casserole. The potatoes should fit the casserole neatly with edges almost touching. Add water to barely cover and salt to taste. Dot with butter and add the oil. Bring to a boil over high heat and simmer five minutes. Place the casserole in the oven and bake about one hour. When done, all of the water should have disappeared and the potatoes should be golden brown on top and bottom. If they are not browned, place the casserole on top of the stove and cook the potatoes turning once until slices are browned top and bottom. Yield: Four to six servings.

Caraway Seed Potatoes

The Sugarplum, Bridgehampton

2 pounds small potatoes
Caraway seeds
Salt
½ cup melted butter

Wash potatoes and cut in half (do not peel). Dip cut potato side in salt and caraway seeds. Place potato salted side down on greased baking sheet and brush with melted butter. Place baking sheet in preheated oven at 350 degrees for about 30 minutes or until done.

Mock French Fries

Pare medium-size potatoes and slice into strips as for French fries. Soak in ice water for about half an hour, drain and dry. Melt one tablespoon of shortening per potato in a large skillet, and add potatoes a few at a time. When they are thoroughly coated, lay them out on a greased cookie sheet, sprinkle with salt and bake in a 450 degree oven for 20 minutes, turning frequently. Brown under broiler for another 10 minutes, and serve hot.

VARIATIONS

POTATO CHEESE STICKS After laying the potatoes on the cookie sheet, sprinkle with onion salt, paprika and monosodium glutamate. Bake 20 to 30 minutes in a 450 degree oven, and sprinkle with Parmesan cheese before serving.

Moisha's Half Baked Potatoes

Cut baking potatoes in half lengthwise. Dot with butter and bake in 350 to 400 degree oven, cut side up, until done, about 25 to 30 minutes. The potatoes will form a puffy browned top and look fancy.

Baked Potato "Chips"

These are even faster. Cut potatoes, unpeeled, into eighths or smaller. Lay out on cookie sheet, cut side up, and bake in 450 degree oven until puffy and crisp.

"Human Nature will not flourish, any more than a potato, if it be planted and replanted, for too long a series of generations, in the same worn-out soil."

Nathaniel Hawthorne (1804-1864) *The Scarlet Letter*

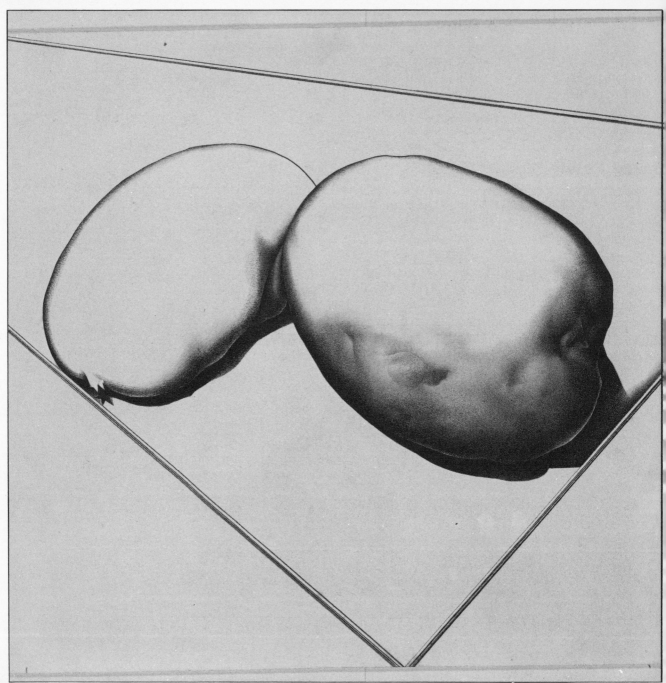

Casserole Potatoes

Potatoes Romanoff

Mrs. Maurice Tarplin, Southampton

4 cups cooked sliced potatoes
1 cup cottage cheese
1 cup dairy sour cream
1 cup American or Cheddar cheese, diced
2 cups milk
2 tablespoons dry minced onions
1 teaspoon garlic salt
Buttered bread crumbs

Mix all ingredients except bread crumbs thoroughly. Pour into buttered casserole, and sprinkle bread crumbs on top. Bake at 350 degrees for one hour. Serves six as a main dish, 12 as a side dish.

Anya's Tatra Potato Pudding

Here is a delicious winter recipe which my mother in Czechoslovakia prepared weekly, while baking bread. It was in a small section called the Tatra Mountains, with a freedom-loving people, now cut off from Czechoslovakia and annexed into the Iron Curtain...I chose this Czech name for the potato pudding so that these poor people will live in our minds in this beautiful free country.

Mrs. Curtis Fremond, Wading River

3 large potatoes, peeled and grated
2 medium-size onions, grated
2 eggs, whole
1/8 teaspoon pepper, freshly-ground
1½ teaspoons of salt, or according to taste
Italian parsley, chopped

Mix these ingredients thoroughly. Before adding eggs, partly drain water out of potatoes. Using a ring form, pour two tablespoons of vegetable oil on bottom of pan to grease thoroughly. Also pour two tablespoons of oil on top of the ingredients. Bake for one hour in 400 degree oven until the top forms a crust. Invert pudding, fill center with creamed chopped spinach or creamed mushrooms. Serves eight.

Anthony's Scalloped Potatoes

My favorite way ot preparing potatoes is this one, for several reasons: flavor; they require no attention; they can be varied by the addition of a spice or single other ingredient.

Anthony's at the Hedges, East Hampton

2 pounds potatoes
1 stick butter (¼ pound)
2 cups milk
1 small onion, finely chopped
Salt and pepper

In a two-quart casserole, place layers of thinly sliced potatoes. Between each layer, dot with butter, some onion, salt and pepper. Pour milk over all. Bake, covered, in preheated 375 degree oven for 45 minutes or until tender.

Most times I add a half-cup of grated cheese.

For variation, add one spice such as chopped chives, basil, curry, nutmeg, mustard or bacon cut in small pieces.

For a one-dish meal, try a ham steak placed as the middle layer in the casserole.

Six-Hour Potatoes In Cream

Squire's Restaurant, East Hampton

Use one Long Island Russet or Idaho potato per person. Peel potatoes and trim edges to make a rough rectangle. Cut potatoes lengthwise and crosswise to make small cubes about one-quarter inch square.

Place potatoes in upper part of a double boiler, or similar arrangement, and add heavy cream to just barely cover them. Season with salt, white pepper, and add one clove of peeled garlic.

Leave space between boiling water and the upper vessel. Simmer potatoes on lowest possible flame for six hours. Stir occasionally. Potatoes will retain their shape and texture, while cream reduces to a delicious consistency.

Skillet Potatoes

Potatoes And Onions Racelle

This dish is quickly prepared and makes a substantial accompaniment for steaks and chops.

1 large boiling potato per person
1 large onion per person
Butter
Salt and pepper

Parboil scrubbed but unpeeled potatoes about eight minutes. Cut potatoes and onions into quarters. Melt butter in skillet and saute potatoes and onions until the potatoes are somewhat mealy and the onions are browned but still a bit crunchy.

Shave 'N' Save

Mary Margaret Goodrich, New York

Save all potato peelings. Fry them with coarsely chopped onions and country sausage, bacon or hot Italian sausage, and some parsley. If you use hot Italian sausage, sprinkle Parmesan cheese on it when served. Or fry them with *anything.*

Caramelized Potatoes

This recipe is Scandinavian and really great at Christmas with turkey or anytime with roast goose or duck.

The Eatery, Poxabogue Golf Course, Bridgehampton

24 small new potatoes
½ cup sugar
8 tablespoons or ¼ pound butter, unsalted

Drop unpeeled potatoes in boiling water and cook 15 to 20 minutes. Drain, let cool and peel.

Melt one-half cup sugar in heavy 10-inch or 12-inch skillet over low heat. Cook slowly three to five minutes, until sugar turns light brown, stirring constantly with wooden spoon. Don't let it get too dark or burn. Stir in melted butter, and as many potatoes as possible without crowding pan.

Shake the pan almost constantly to roll and coat them on all sides. Remove the hot, caramelized potatoes to a heated serving dish and repeat the procedure until all the potatoes are coated. They may be served right away or kept warm in a slow oven for no more than 15 minutes. Serves eight.

Pears And Potatoes

2 tablespoons butter
1 onion, chopped
2 tablespoons flour
1½ cups water
Salt
Brown sugar
Cinnamon
4 cooking pears, medium size
6 potatoes, pared

Brown onion and flour in two tablespoons of fat. Add water, cook, stirring until smooth, and add salt, sugar and cinnamon to taste. Slice pears and potatoes into quarters, add them to the sauce, and cook until tender, about 25 minutes. This is good with roasted meat or poultry and a light green salad.

Crusty New Potatoes

Miriam Mednick, Philadelphia

12-16 new potatoes, depending on size
½ cup chicken fat or butter
2 cloves garlic, crushed
Salt and pepper to taste

Boil potatoes in their jackets. Peel. Melt fat, add garlic and peeled, seasoned potatoes. Saute over medium heat until potatoes are browned on all sides. Turn potatoes gently so the crust doesn't break as they are browning. Delicious with roasts and chicken. For four people.

One medium-sized white potato provides 33 milligrams of vitamin C. as much as a glass of tomato juice, and 1.5 milligrams of iron, or as much as is found in an egg.

Potato Curry

¼ cup butter
1 cup chopped onions
5 cups potatoes, peeled and sliced
1½ teaspoons turmeric
¼ teaspoon powdered ginger
½ teaspoon freshly ground pepper
3 tomatoes
1 pound small fresh peas or 1 package frozen
  petite peas
2 cups boiling water
1½ teaspoons salt
2 tablespoons lemon juice
2 tablespoons parsley, finely chopped

Saute the onions in butter until golden brown.
Add potatoes, turmeric, ginger and pepper, and
continue to saute, stirring, for a few minutes
longer. Chop the tomatoes, add to vegetables,
and simmer for about eight to 10 minutes. Add
peas and boiling water, raise heat slightly, and
cook until peas are tender, about five minutes.
Add salt and lemon juice and garnish with
chopped parsley. Four servings.

NOTE This is also a delicious filling for Middle
Eastern *pita* bread, as a luncheon sandwich.

Potatoes Italian Style

2 pounds new potatoes
3 tablespoons olive oil
2 cloves garlic
2 tablespoons chopped fresh oregano, or 1
  teaspoon dried oregano
6 ripe tomatoes
6 tablespoons butter
Salt
Freshly-ground pepper

Boil potatoes until tender, drain, peel and slice.
Heat olive oil in a saucepan until moderately hot,
and crush garlic through a garlic press into the oil.
Cook for about a minute, then add tomatoes,
oregano and seasoning. Simmer 15 minutes.
Meanwhile, brown sliced potatoes in butter until
golden on both sides. Add tomato mixture and
toss gently. Taste for seasoning, and serve in
warm dish. A colorful accompaniment for fish or
veal.

Potato Pancakes Milwaukee Style

These pancakes are thin and crisp, and especially good with poultry and poultry gravy.

Elaine Ewing, Sagaponack

2 cups raw grated potatoes
2 whole eggs
1½ teaspoons salt
1 tablespoon flour (rounded), or bread crumbs may be substituted
1 tablespoon finely chopped onion
½ cup boiling milk

Mix all ingredients together well and bake on greased griddle.

Scallion Potatoes

Pare and thinly slice three medium-size potatoes. Heat one-quarter cup butter or vegetable oil in skillet, add potatoes and eight thinly sliced scallions. Season with one teaspoon salt, freshly ground pepper and one-quarter teaspoon celery salt. Stir gently and saute over low heat until browned, scraping particles from bottom, for about 25 minutes. Serves four.

My Grandmother's Kugel

Sarah Kugelman, New York City [Age 9]

First take a potato and grate it in a bowl but peel off the brown stuff then pour out the extra water then get an onion and just grate it two times then crack an egg. Then put bread crumbs in and salt. you want pepper, you can put it in then mix it. Put oil in a pan and let it boil, then put potato pancake in and when it boils turn it over and then cook a little while and there it is.

close your eyes my little baby...

Reynold Ruffins

47

Mashed Potatoes

Cream Cheese Potatoes

Liza Werner, Sag Harbor

Boil until cooked five pounds of potatoes. Fry in skillet until lightly browned three large chopped onions, two cloves of garlic, two large chopped leeks, parsley, salt and pepper. (If no leeks are available, add two more onions.)

Peel and mash the potatoes. Add browned onions, leeks and garlic. Add one-half pound butter, one and one-half cups freshly grated Parmesan cheese, and one large package of cream cheese. Blend thoroughly.

Oil pan and shake into it some seasoned bread crumbs. Add potato mixture and flatten evenly into pan. Beat an egg and spread on top of mixture. Bake at 325 degrees until hot and lightly browned.

Colcannon

This is a classic Irish potato dish.

2   pounds medium-size potatoes
½   pound cabbage, kale or spinach
2   strips bacon
2   tablespoons butter
1   teaspoon minced onion
½   teaspoon salt
⅛   teaspoon pepper

Boil or steam potatoes until soft, peel and mash. Shred cabbage, kale or spinach and cook, covered, with bacon and one-half cup water until very tender. Drain and sieve through strainer or food mill. Melt butter in a large saucepan. Add minced onion, salt and pepper, potatoes and cabbage. Blend thoroughly and heat. Serves six.

Champ

Another classic Irish dish is this way of combining vegetables with hot mashed potatoes. Mix either peas, chives or sauteed onions, spinach or cabbage into hot mashed potatoes. Make a depression in the center of each serving and fill with melted butter. Dip each forkful into the butter before eating. (It is a painless way to get children to eat their vegetables, too.)

Spinach Tarts

4 cups rich mashed potatoes
2 tablespoons butter
3 cups spinach, sauteed in butter
2 eggs, well beaten

Using mashed potatoes which have been creamed with egg yolk, cream and seasoning, form six cups or shells and place on a greased baking dish. Fill with spinach and brush with beaten egg. Brown in 450 to 500 degree oven for about five minutes.

Orange Potatoes

6 medium potatoes
2 tablespoons butter
⅔ cup milk, heated
1 teaspoon salt
Juice of one orange
Rind of one orange, grated

Preheat oven to 350 degrees. Boil potatoes in their skins until tender, drain, peel and mash well. Add butter, milk, salt and orange juice and beat until fluffy. Turn into greased baking dish, top with orange rind, and bake for about 15 minutes. Serves four. Nice with fowl.

Alice Williamson's Swedish Green Potatoes

Helen Rattray, Amagansett

Boil six large potatoes, about three pounds. When tender, peel and put through ricer. Add three-quarters cup light cream, one teaspoon sugar, one-quarter pound butter, two teaspoons salt, one-quarter teaspoon pepper. Beat until light and fluffy. Add two tablespoons fresh chopped dill leaves (or one and one-half tablespoons dried dill leaves) and one package of frozen chopped spinach which has been cooked according to directions on package and seasoned to taste. Beat again until mixture is blended. Check for seasoning. Place in one and one-half quart greased casserole. Bake 20 minutes at 400 degrees. It isn't necessary to use the ricer if you have an electric mixer to mash the potatoes. Should serve six.

Barbara Nessim 1971

Potato Souffle

4 medium potatoes, boiled and peeled and drained
4 tablespoons butter
1 cup sour cream
1 teaspoon salt
½ teaspoon pepper
3 egg yolks, well beaten
3 egg whites, beaten until stiff

Mash potatoes and beat in butter, sour cream and seasonings. Blend in beaten egg yolks, then fold in egg whites until mixture is fluffy. Turn into one and one-half quart buttered souffle or baking dish and bake at 350 degrees for 20 minutes. Serve at once. Four to six servings.

Potato Yorkshire Pudding

6 medium potatoes
½ cup hot milk, scant
1 bouillon cube
3 tablespoons melted butter
1 teaspoon salt
¼ teaspoon pepper
1 or 2 eggs, lightly beaten
½ teaspoon paprika

Boil potatoes, then mash. Dissolve bouillon cube in hot milk, add butter, salt and pepper, and beat into potatoes. Set aside one and one-half tablespoons of the egg. Add the remainder to the potato mixture and beat again. Put mixture into well-buttered eight-inch or nine-inch cake pan. Brush with remaining egg mixed with paprika. Put in 400 degree oven until brown. Serve in wedges. Six to eight servings.

Potato Croquettes

12 potatoes
6 tablespoons butter
6 egg yolks
Nutmeg
Flour
2 whole eggs
2 cups breadcrumbs, ground fresh
Peanut oil
Salt and freshly ground pepper

Boil the potatoes in salt water until soft when pierced, then peel and mash. Add butter, egg yolks, a dash of nutmeg and season to taste. Roll the mixture into small cones or balls and dust lightly with flour. Beat eggs, and dip the cones into the egg then breadcrumbs. Heat oil to 375 degrees in a deep skillet or pot, and fry the croquettes until golden brown.

Vegetable-Potato Pancakes

1 pound cold boiled potatoes, peeled
½ ounce melted butter
2 spring onions, finely chopped
2 large tomatoes, peeled and chopped
2 ounces flour
Salt and pepper
Olive oil

Mash the potatoes and mix with the butter, onions, tomatoes, flour, seasoning. Knead gently and roll out to three-quarter inch thickness. Cut into rounds with a cookie cutter or small juice glass, and fry quickly in very hot olive oil, or bake on a greased cookie sheet at 400 degrees, until golden brown.

Potato Dumplings I

The Sugarplum, Bridgehampton

1½ pounds boiled potatoes
1 pound raw potatoes
1 egg
2 ounces flour
1 teaspoon salt

Wash potatoes and boil them. Peel boiled potatoes and rice them right away. Place in bowl and let them cool for a few hours in refrigerator. Peel raw potatoes and grate them very fine.
Press them through a cloth and mix them with the riced boiled potatoes. Add to mixture the egg, flour and salt. Dust your hands with flour and form fist-size balls. Drop dumplings in salted boiling water and simmer for 20 minutes on low heat.

To rescue oversalted food cooked in water, drop in a few slices of raw potato and boil until the excess salt is absorbed.

Potato Dumplings II

Kay Zachary, Amagansett

To about 3 cups boiled, shaken dry, peeled
   potatoes add:
¾ teaspoon salt
¼ cup farina
⅓ cup flour

Beat one egg with three teaspoons milk and add to mixture. Hold bowl over several quarts of boiling water and slice off pieces of dough, letting them slide into water. Simmer 10 minutes and they will rise to the top. Skim off with a slotted spoon. Place into a skillet in which you have browned about one cup bread crumbs and either add dark brown fried onions on top when serving or serve hot cooked prunes or hot cherries on the side. Either fruit is very good with this dish. I suggest the prunes be cooked not only with water and sugar but also a good amount of sherry and several thin lemon slices.

Filled Potato Dumplings

4 medium-sized potatoes
1 egg yolk
4 ounces flour
1 small onion, chopped
Salt and pepper
2 ounces ham, chopped
1 ounce butter

Boil potatoes in their skins. Peel and mash. Mix with flour and egg yolk until smooth, and season to taste. Brown the chopped onion and ham in butter. Roll out potato dough to half-inch thickness, and cut into rounds with a juice glass or cookie cutter. Spread the onion-ham mixture on half the rounds, cover each with the remaining ones, and pinch edges together to seal. Drop into boiling water, and remove with a slotted spoon when they rise to the surface. Serve with melted butter.
VARIATION For a sweet version of this use prune jam in place of the ham-onion mixture. Sprinkle with sugar and cinnamon and serve with melted butter.

Sauerkraut Dumplings

Here is a recipe I use a lot.

Mrs. Edward Richardson, Sag Harbor

Mix well one cup cold mashed potatoes and one egg. Add one-half cup flour. Make a stiff dough and roll out. Cut in small squares and drop in the top of boiling sauerkraut.

Potato Gnocchi

6 baking potatoes
3 egg yolks
2 teaspoons salt
2 to 2½ cups flour

Bake or boil potatoes until tender. Peel, mash and chill in refrigerator for several hours or overnight. Stir in egg yolks and salt, mix well and turn onto lightly floured board. Make a depression in the center of the potato mixture, and put in one cup of flour. Knead thoroughly, adding more flour as needed, until a smooth, elastic dough is achieved. Roll the dough into frankfurter shapes, and slice each into one-inch segments.

Press thumb into each segment to curl edges of dough. Drop gnocchi into about four quarts of fully boiling water, lightly salted. Lower heat and cook gently, uncovered, about three to five minutes or until gnocchi rise to the surface. Remove the gnocchi with a slotted spoon. Serve with melted butter and grated cheese, or with marinara or other pasta sauce.

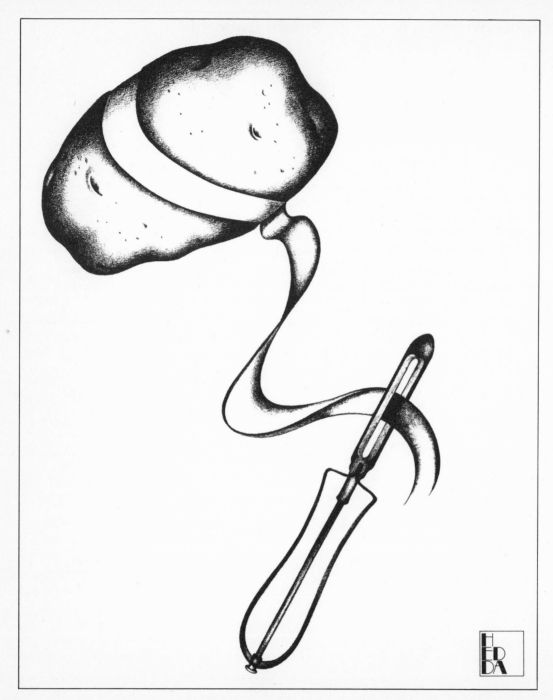

Potato Knishes

DOUGH

2 cups all-purpose flour
¼ teaspoon salt
½ cup water
1 tablespoon oil
1 whole egg
1 egg white

Sift flour and salt in a mound on a board. Make a hole in the middle and drop in the whole egg and additional egg white. Use your fingertips and start working the mixture together. Add water and oil gradually and continue mixing (still with fingertips) until all the flour is worked in. At this point the dough should be smooth and sticky. Slap the dough vigorously with the palm of your hand as if you are bouncing a ball. Stretch it up and slap it down again until the dough is no longer sticky, perhaps 100 times. Shape into a smooth ball, brush with a little oil and cover with a warm bowl. Let stand 20 to 30 minutes. Spread a clean tablecloth on a large table. Sprinkle cloth with flour and put the ball of dough in the center. With a rolling pin, roll into a large circle. Now stretch the dough with your hands in a gentle hand-over-hand motion, moving around the table as you stretch the dough evenly. When thin as parchment, trim off all thick edges with scissors and sprinkle the entire surface lightly with oil.

FILLING

4 cups cooked mashed potatoes
⅓ cup finely chopped onion
⅓ cup chicken fat or Nyafat
Salt and pepper

Saute onion in chicken fat until limp, stir into potatoes and season with salt and pepper.

Shape the potato filling into a roll about two inches in diameter and as long as the dough is wide. Put filling on the edge of the dough nearest you and lift the cloth with both hands, rolling dough over and over the potato filling.

Now with a sawing motion, using the side of your hand, break the roll into slices about one and one-half inches wide. This gives the ragged edge which is traditional. Place on a greased baking pan and put in preheated 425 degree oven until crisp and brown. Serve with pot roast or stew.

Potato Blintzes

Mrs. Yetta Seldon, Bayonne, New Jersey

1 cup sifted flour
2 eggs
1 cup water
½ teaspoon salt
1 tablespoon sugar

Beat the eggs, and add sugar and salt. Add the flour and water alternately, beating well. The batter should be thin, just enough to coat the frying pan. You can use two pans at the same time, greased lightly and kept hot each time the batter is poured into it. If too much batter slips into the pan, pour the excess back. Fry only one side, just enough to cook but not brown. Then turn pancake fried side up onto a clean towel or cloth. These may be filled immediately or packed in waxed paper and frozen.

FILLING Boil four or five potatoes, peel and mash. Saute onion, with drained mushrooms if desired. Mash potatoes with onions and mushrooms and salt to taste. Beat in one egg and enough milk to make a smooth mixture. Place a few tablespoons of this mixture on the cooked side of each pancake and fold like an envelope. Saute in buttered pan for about one-half hour. Serve with sour cream.

Potato Waffles

1 cup sifted flour
2 teaspoons baking powder
1 teaspoon salt
2 eggs, beaten
1 cup milk
5 tablespoons melted butter
1½ cups mashed cooked potatoes
¼ cup minced onion

Sift together dry ingredients. Combine remaining ingredients, mix well, and add to first mixture. Beat with whisk, rotary or electric beater until thoroughly blended.
Use three-quarters cup of batter for each waffle, baking in a hot waffle iron for three or four minutes or until no longer steaming. This will make four large waffles.

Mashed Potato Noodles

1½ pounds potatoes, cooked, peeled and mashed
1 tablespoon butter
2½ cups flour
1 teaspoon salt
3 eggs, beaten

Blend butter into warm mashed potatoes. Add flour and salt gradually. Add eggs and stir until a soft, sticky dough is formed. Roll out onto a lightly floured board and cut into strips one-quarter inch wide and two inches long. Cook in rapidly boiling water for about ten minutes. Serve plain with butter or sauce, or toss with cottage cheese or fried onions.

Potato-Apple Stuffing For Goose

1 pound tart apples
1 pound yellow onions
1 pound potatoes,
Rind of 1 orange, grated
¼ cup orange juice
Water
Thyme, parsley, sage
Salt and pepper

Core, peel and slice apples thinly. Slice onions the same way. Put into saucepan with orange juice and enough water to cover. All sprigs of fresh herbs or dried chopped herbs in a cheesecloth bag, salt and pepper to taste, and cook until apples and onions are tender. Meanwhile, boil, peel, mash and season potatoes well. When apples and onions are done, remove herbs and puree through sieve or food mill. Add grated orange rind and enough potato to make a firm stuffing and mix well. Stuff the goose just before roasting.

Liver-Potato Poultry Stuffing

3 pounds potatoes, boiled and peeled
4 tablespoons rendered poultry fat or butter
Liver from poultry, diced
1 onion, diced
salt and pepper

Mash potatoes while still hot. Saute diced liver and onion in hot fat or butter until golden, then mix contents of skillet into the potatoes. Season to taste. Yields five to six cups stuffing, or enough for a 10-pound turkey.

Potato "Brioche"

Here is an ingenious way to prepare leftover mashed potatoes so that they look like the little French rolls called *brioches*.

Leftover mashed potatoes
Egg yolk
Flour

Mix egg yolk into leftover mashed potatoes. Lightly flour a pastry board and flatten the potato mixture to a one-inch thickness. Using a small glass or cookie cutter, cut out rounds to form the base of the brioche. Make a depression in each with your thumb. Roll an equal number of small balls, about one inch in diameter, and use them to top the depressions. Brush all over with egg yolk, and bake in a 350 degree oven until golden brown. These can be made ahead and reheated.

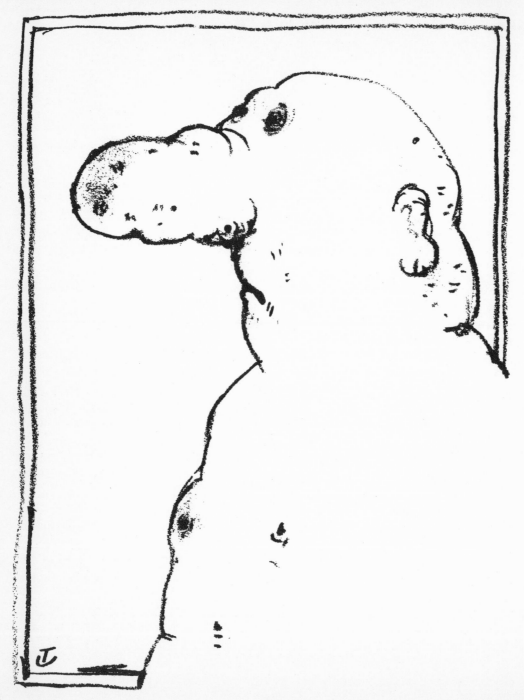

Main Dishes

Potato Omelet I

Mary Heming, North Haven

FILLING (*for three omelets*) Take approximately three cups of peeled, cubed potatoes.

Put a few spoonsful of bacon fat or olive oil into a skillet, heat and add potatoes, stirring occasionally to prevent sticking. Sprinkle with kosher salt. Meanwhile, peel an onion and slice (more than one if desired). When potatoes are about half cooked, add sliced onions, and partially cover the skillet to allow them to cook through and retain some moisture without making them soggy. Peel a clove of garlic, mince it, and add to potatoes and onions just before the end of cooking. Grind a little black pepper to taste. Remove skillet from stove and set aside.

OMELET Make each omelet individually, using two eggs for each. Break eggs into small dish and beat with fork, not an egg beater, just enough so that egg is combined but still "ropey." After eggs are mixed, put one generous tablespoon of butter into a cured omelet pan over medium high heat. When the bubbling has subsided, pour in the eggs, and immediately start pulling eggs from the edge to the center, tipping the pan to fill empty edges with uncooked egg, and shaking gently to keep omelet moving in the pan, until eggs reach desired dryness. Then put heat down to low, continuing to shake pan. Lay potato mixture onto eggs, then slip onto plate, flipping half of the omelet over potatoes to cover them.

Potato Omelet II

Ely's Steak House, East Hampton

1 cup plus 3 tablespoons olive oil
3 large potatoes (about 2 pounds), peeled and
   sliced into ⅛-inch thick rounds
2 teaspoons salt
½ cup finely chopped onions
4 eggs

In a heavy 10-inch or 12-inch skillet, heat one cup of olive oil over high heat until hot but not smoking. Add the potatoes, sprinkle them with one teaspoon of the salt and turn them about in the pan to coat them well with oil. Continue cooking, turning occasionally, until the potatoes brown lightly. Then add the onions, reduce the heat and cook for about 10 minutes, stirring every now and then until the potatoes and onions are tender. Transfer the entire contents of the skillet to a large sieve or colander and drain off excess oil. With a whisk or rotary or electric beater, beat eggs and remaining teaspoon of salt until frothy. Gently stir in the potatoes and onions. Heat the remaining three tablespoons of oil in a heavy eight-inch skillet until a light haze forms above it. Pour in the omelet mixture, spread it out with a spatula and cook over a moderate heat for two minutes.

Shake the pan periodically to keep eggs from sticking. When the omelet is firm but not dry, cover the skillet with a flat plate and, grasping the plate and skillet firmly together, invert them and turn the omelet out into the plate. Then carefully slide the omelet back into the pan. Cook for three minutes longer to brown the under side. Serve at once. Makes four to six portions.

NOTE Sausage may be added also if desired.

Cold Potato Omelet

This is a favorite recipe from Spain and makes a
   delightful summer lunch.

Miriam Mednick, Philadelphia

4 potatoes, boiled and diced
6 eggs
Salt and pepper

Beat eggs lightly. Make omelet in butter. Fill
omelet with potatoes, season and fold. Refrigerate
and serve cold in wedges.

Oeufs Au Nid (Eggs In The Nest)

Miriam Mednick, Philadelphia

3 medium onions, sliced
3 medium potatoes, cooked and diced
6 eggs
butter
bread crumbs
salt and pepper

Boil potatoes, dice into one-half-inch or one-inch
cubes. Saute onion rings in butter until they are
transparent. Add potatoes, salt and pepper.
Put in low-sided baking dish. Preheat oven to 350
degrees. Make "nests" in the onion-potato
mixture and break eggs into the nests. Season to
taste with salt and pepper, dot liberally with butter
and sprinkle with bread crumbs. Bake until the
eggs are set, approximately 15 minutes. Serve in
wedges. Especially good for lunch or Sunday
brunch.

Pennsylvania Dutch Scrapple

2 tablespoons shortening or vegetable oil
1 medium size onion
2 tablespoons chopped green pepper
½ teaspoon salt
¼ teaspoon pepper
3 medium potatoes, diced
1 tomato, diced
4 egg yolks
4 egg whites

Melt shortening in large skillet over low heat. Saute
onion and pepper until soft. Add potatoes and
seasonings, cover and simmer for 20 minutes. Add
tomato and mix well. Beat egg yolks with a whisk
until they are light. Beat whites until just stiff. Fold
yolks into whites, then fold both into the skillet
mixture. Recover, and bake in 350 degree oven
until eggs are cooked and the top is lightly
browned, about 20 minutes. Serves four.

Lobster Pots

4 large baking potatoes, baked
6 ounces lobster, fresh cooked or canned
½ cup butter
½ cup light cream
1 teaspoon salt
⅛ teaspoon cayenne pepper
4 teaspoons grated onion
1 cup grated yellow cheese, sharp or mild
½ teaspoon paprika

Halve baked potatoes lengthwise, scoop out potato and beat with butter, cream, salt, cayenne, onion and cheese. Fold in lobster and pile into shells. Sprinkle with paprika and brown under broiler or in 450 degree oven for about 15 minutes. Serves four.

NOTE Canned tuna or salmon also may be substituted for the lobster.

Fishing Boats

4 large baking potatoes, baked
1 cup milk
½ cup clam juice
2 stalks celery, diced fine
2 slices onion, diced fine
2 tablespoons flour
2 tablespoons butter
Salt and pepper
Paprika
3 dozen clams or oysters (or an equivalent amount of mussels or diced fish)

Cut baked potatoes lengthwise and scoop out the center of each half. Combine the milk and clam juice in the top of a double boiler and heat to scalding point. Add diced celery and onion. Cream flour and butter, then add to mixture, and season to taste. Lower heat slightly and stir constantly with a wire whisk until the mixture thickens. Add clams or fish and scooped-out potato, cook gently until tender, then remove from heat. Stuff into potato shells, dot with paprika and serve at once.

Fish-And-Potato Hash

4 tablespoons olive oil or butter
½ pound potatoes, peeled and diced
1 pound fish fillets
½ cup flour
¼ cup tomato sauce
1 tablespoon chopped parsley
Salt and pepper to taste

Heat the olive oil or butter in a large skillet and saute the potatoes until nicely browned. Slice the fish fillets into one-inch squares, flour and season them well. Move the potatoes to the skillet edge, reduce heat slightly and saute the fish until tender and flaky. Remove to a warm platter. Add tomato sauce and parsley to the pan, heat well, and pour over fish hash. Serve with buttered broccoli or asparagus.

Fish Pie

Years ago the *Brooklyn Eagle* gave $1.00 for any recipe they used. I won on this one.

Mrs. Washington White, Greenport

1 cup flaked fish
2 cups riced potatoes
½ cup cracker crumbs
1 egg, lightly beaten
½ cup milk
2 tablespoons butter or margarine
¼ cup grated cheese

Mix potatoes, fish and milk. Put in greased pie tin. Spread with egg. Cover with cracker crumbs mixed with butter. Sprinkle with cheese. Bake 12 minutes in 350 degree oven.

It would take nine to 12 pounds of potatoes to fulfill a person's minimum daily calorie requirements.

Papas Rellenas

The House on Otter Pond, Sag Harbor

Boil 12 medium potatoes. When still warm, peel, mash and add enough butter for mashed potato consistency. Then add cornmeal, little by little, until mixture is like dough.
Meanwhile, to make the sauce, chop one-quarter pound of fatback, sliver three cloves of garlic, and fry in one-quarter cup of olive oil. Remove garlic and fatback when brown. Chop 12 pitted green olives and three medium onions. Add to oil, along with one-half cup raisins, salt and pepper. Add tomato sauce to cover well, and simmer for 20 minutes. Add one-half pound of chopped meat and stir until cooked.
Dust hands with cornmeal, take some potato dough and make a small pancake. Holding the pancake in one hand, make a depression in the center using the other fist (similar to the catcher's mitt gesture). Insert sauce and enclose it into a ball, so that it looks like a potato again. Fry in 375 degree oil until golden. These can be prepared ahead, and reheated either by frying or in the oven. Serve with poultry or fish.

Senora Mojica's Stuffed Potatoes

The following recipe was sent to us by our 14-year-old correspondent from a small village near Bogota, Colombia.

Our best way is stuffed potatoes. We wash them. Then cut off a piece on the top and scoop out the inside and stuff as follows: rice, green peas, carrots, ground meat, a hard-boiled egg chopped up in tiny pieces with cheese added. This mixture is first cooked together with garlic spice and a pinch of salt; then stuffed into the potatoes. The piece at the top is replaced and secured with toothpicks. then prepare a thick sauce for the potatoes, chopping up tomatoes, cheese, butter and onions cooked in enough milk to make a sauce. Then everything is ready to serve. This is the way my mother prepares them.

Agobardo Mojica

Red Flannel Hash

This classic New England dish makes leftover corned beef something special.

1 tablespoon butter or shortening
1 cup chopped cooked corned beef
3 cups chopped boiled potatoes
1 cup chopped cooked beets
½ cup chopped onion
Cream (optional)

Combined chopped corned beef and potatoes, moistening with a small amount of cream if dry. Add beets and onion and mix well. Heat butter or shortening in a heavy skillet until bubbles have subsided, then spread mixture evenly in the pan and brown slowly until crust forms on bottom. Turn as you would an omelet, brown other side and turn onto hot platter. Cut into wedges. Serves four.
A watercress salad is a good accompaniment.

Lamb And Potato Moussaka

This is an adaptation of a recipe from Paula Peck's cookbook. It is unbelievably tasty.

Nora Ephron Greenburg, East Hampton

3½ pounds leg of lamb cut into cubes
⅔ cup tomato puree
2 large onions, chopped
2 cloves garlic, minced
1 teaspoon basil
2 teaspoons salt
Pepper
½ cup chopped parsley
3 pounds potatoes, peeled and cut into matchsticks
¼ cup olive oil
½ cup Parmesan cheese

Combine all ingredients except potatoes and oil, and mix. Place in a big shallow container (if possible, wider at the top than the bottom; a paella dish is perfect). Press mixture down. Sprinkle with Parmesan. Then arrange potatoes on top of meat and sprinkle them with oil. Place in a 400 degree oven for one and one-half hours, basting potatoes with juices from casserole. Serve when the potatoes are very crisp. This should be served immediately, but it can be held for a bit at a low temperature. Serves six.

Russian Steppes

This adventurous combination of ingredients is not uncommon to Russian cuisine.

4 medium size potatoes, baked, peeled and sliced
3 pickled herrings, chopped
6 ounces salami, sliced thinly
¼ pint sour cream
4 ounces breadcrumbs

Butter a casserole or deep baking dish. Put a layer of sliced potatoes around the bottom, then alternate with a layer of herring, another layer of potatoes, a layer of sausage, again potatoes, and so on until the ingredients are used up, ending with a layer of potatoes. Spread sour cream on each layer, and salt and pepper to taste. Top generously with breadcrumbs and dot with butter. Bake in 350 degree oven for about 40 minutes or until potatoes are browned and tender.

Shepherd's Pie

This is a delicious way to serve leftover lamb.

3 cups cubed cooked lamb
3 cups gravy, leftover or prepared
2 tablespoons minced onion
½ cup thinly sliced celery
1 clove garlic, minced
2 tablespoons butter
½ cup chopped parsley
3 egg yolks, beaten
1 egg white
3 cups mashed potatoes
Freshly ground black pepper

Saute onion, celery and garlic in butter for about 10 minutes until soft and transparent. Stir in lamb, gravy, parsley and pepper. Add egg yolks to potatoes and mix well. Line the sides of a small casserole with the potato, which should be of a fairly stiff consistency. Brush the inner wall with egg white. Pour in lamb mixture. Spoon remaining potatoes around the top. Bake in 350 degree oven for half an hour.

Ham And Potato Casserole

1½ pounds cooked ham, diced
6 raw potatoes, peeled and sliced
4 green peppers, seeded and cut into strips
2 large onions, sliced
½ pint milk
1 egg
4 ounces grated cheese
Salt
Freshly ground pepper
Butter

Butter a baking dish, then cover bottom with a layer of potatoes, top with a layer of onions, a layer of peppers and a layer of ham. Repeat until the dish is filled, ending with a layer of potatoes. Beat egg with milk, season to taste, and add to casserole. Dot with butter and bake at 350 degrees for one and one-half hours. Sprinkle with grated cheese and return to oven or place under broiler to brown. Four to six servings.

Potatoes Boheme

4 large baking potatoes
½ pound sausage meat
1 egg

Scrub potatoes and parboil in skins. Slit skin lengthwise, and remove inside with teaspoon, leaving shell about one-half inch thick. Stuff carefully with sausage meat until whole looking. Brush with beaten egg and bake in 400 degree oven for 20 minutes.

Pig-In-A-Poke Potatoes

1 or 2 medium potatoes per person
Equal number of cocktail frankfurters or small
   sausages
Sliced bacon or salt pork
Pepper

Scrub potatoes or pare. Using an apple corer, cut a hole through the center of each, and fill with a small sausage or frankfurter. Put potatoes in a shallow baking dish and cover with slices of bacon or salt pork. Bake at 400 degrees for about 50 minutes or until tender. Baste with hot water and drippings when necessary.

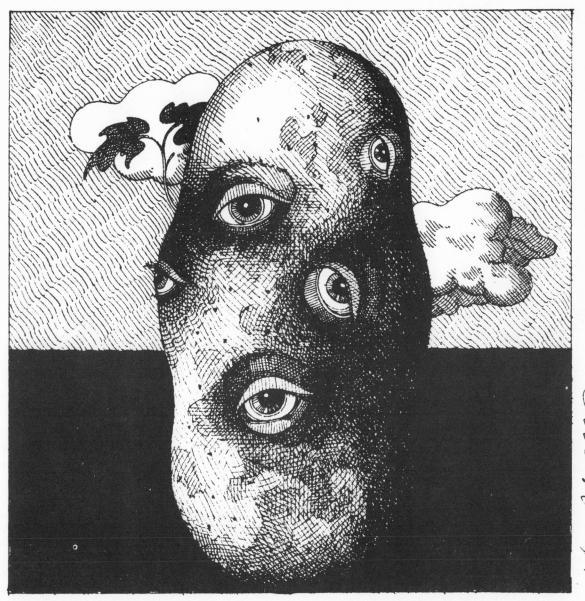

Breads, Cakes, Cookies

Flowerpot Bread

This healthful bread calls for baking in flowerpots either new or thoroughly washed in an automatic dishwasher. It makes a delectable conversation piece and an unusual house gift, pot and all.

1 large potato, peeled and diced
1 teaspoon salt
1 cup water
½ cup butter
½ cup sugar
½ cup powdered skim milk
3 eggs, beaten
2 packages yeast
¼ cup warm water
1 teaspoon sugar
5 cups flour, more or less
(or ½ cup soy flour and ¼ cup wheat germ may
   be substituted for part of the flour)

Put potato into water with salt and boil until tender. Remove from heat, add butter and sugar to water, and mash all together. Blend in the powdered milk and beaten eggs. Dissolve yeast in warm water with sugar, and add to mixture. Slowly add flour until a soft dough is achieved. Knead until dough is smooth and elastic, then put into a well-buttered bowl, turn once, cover with a damp cloth, and allow to rise until doubled in bulk. Punch down, knead again, and store covered in the refrigerator until needed. It will last up to 10 days. Before using, allow dough to rise at room temperature for about two hours. Then butter the pots, line with wax paper, butter the paper and fill about two-thirds full with dough. Allow dough to rise. Preheat oven to 400 degrees. Bake at this temperature for 10 minutes, lower heat to 325 degrees and continue baking until done, about one-half to three-quarters of an hour.

White Potato Bread

Hattie G. Aldrich, Riverhead

3 medium potatoes, peeled and sliced
3 cups unsalted water
1 package yeast
2 tablespoons sugar
2 tablespoons shortening
1 tablespoon salt
6 cups flour, approximately

Boil potatoes in water until tender. Mash in the water. Add sugar, shortening and salt, and cool until lukewarm. Dissolve yeast in one-quarter cup warm water. Add softening yeast to first mixture, stir in flour and knead well, adding more flour if necessary.
Place in large greased bowl, turn once so that greased side of dough is on top, cover and let rise in warm place until doubled in bulk. Punch down and let rise 10 minutes. Divide into two greased loaf pans and let rise again until doubled. Bake in 350 degree oven 45 to 50 minutes.

Potatoes will slice easily if the knife is sharp and dipped first into boiling water.

Refrigerator Rolls

This is an old recipe from my mother's family. She says the potato keeps the dough extra moist. They last four days or so in the refrigerator, if you can stand to wait that long.

Our holiday sweet roll was always made by pressing out a rectangle of this dough (jelly roll style) and covering it with brown sugar, dobs of butter, pecan or walnut pieces and a sprinkling of cinnamon; then it was rolled, cut into disks and placed into baking pans, let rise, and baked as in the recipe.

Margaret Miller, Sag Harbor

1 yeast cake
½ cup lukewarm water
⅔ cup shortening
½ cup sugar
4 cups flour, more or less,
 enough to make a stiff dough
1 teaspoon salt
1 cup mashed potatoes
1 cup scalded milk
2 eggs, well beaten

Dissolve yeast in water; add shortening, sugar, salt and freshly mashed potatoes to scalded milk (or some of the potato water). When cold, add yeast. Mix thoroughly and add the eggs. Stir in enough flour to make a stiff dough. Turn out on a lightly floured board and knead well. Pat into bowl large enough to allow for slight rising. Brush with melted butter, cover tightly and place in refrigerator. About an hour before baking, shape as desired, cover and let rise until light. Bake at 400 degrees for 15 to 20 minutes.

Marshall Field's
Famous Potato Flour Muffins

⅛ teaspoon salt
4 eggs beaten separately
1 tablespoon sugar
½ cup potato flour
1 teaspoon baking powder
2 tablespoons ice water

Beat whites of eggs with salt until very stiff and dry. Add sugar to beaten egg yolks until thick and light. Fold whites into yolks. Sift flour and baking powder twice and mix well. Stir in ice water. Pour into greased muffin tins and bake in 375 degree oven 15 to 20 minutes. Makes 12 muffins.

Onion-Potato Muffins

2 egg yolks, beaten
3 cups grated, drained raw potatoes
4 tablespoons grated onion
½ cup sifted flour
1 teaspoon salt
½ teaspoon baking powder
3 tablespoons melted butter
2 egg whites, stiffly beaten

Stir beaten egg yolks into the potatoes. Add onion, flour, salt, baking powder and melted butter. Fold in egg whites. Fill greased muffins tins two-thirds full. Bake at 400 degrees 20 to 25 minutes. Makes one dozen muffins.

Potato-Cornmeal Muffins

2 tablespoons butter
1 tablespoon sugar
2 eggs, beaten
¾ cup milk
1 cup mashed potatoes
1 cup coarse cornmeal
1 tablespoon baking powder
½ teaspoon salt

Cream butter and sugar. Add eggs, milk and mashed potatoes, and mix until well blended. Combine cornmeal, baking powder and salt, and add to first mixture. Stir just enough to moisten dry ingredients, then fill greased muffin tins two-thirds full. Bake at 400 degrees for about 20 minutes or until golden brown. Makes one dozen muffins.

Potato Doughnuts

1 cup mashed potatoes
1 cup sugar
2 tablespoons melted shortening
2 eggs, well beaten
1 teaspoon vanilla
½ cup evaporated milk
½ cup water
½ teaspoon salt
4 teaspoons baking powder
½ teaspoon nutmeg
1 cup sifted flour

Cream sugar and shortening. Add potatoes, eggs, milk, water and vanilla. Combine dry ingredients and blend well with first mixture, adding more flour if needed to make a soft dough. Roll on lightly floured board to one-quarter inch thickness, and cut with floured doughnut cutter. Fry four or five at a time in deep fat heated to 365 degrees. As soon as they rise to the surface, turn them. Fry for about two minutes or until well browned. Drain on paper towels. Makes about two dozen doughnuts. Serve plain, or roll in confectioners sugar, granulated sugar or sugar-and-cinnamon mixture.

Potato Pie Crust

This is a good pie crust for hearty fillings of meat, fish or chicken.

1 cup sifted flour
½ teaspoon salt
½ teaspoon sugar
½ cup cold mashed potatoes
 without seasoning, butter or milk
6 tablespoons solid shortening

Resift flour with salt and sugar. Blend in potatoes with a fork until mealy. Add shortening, cutting in with pastry blender or two knives until mixture consists of small crumbs. Form pastry into a ball, put into plastic bag and chill in refrigerator for about half an hour. Then roll out dough on lightly floured board to one-eighth inch thickness. Press into eight-inch pie pan, trim edges, prick in several places and bake at 400 degrees for 10 to 12 minutes. Allow crust to cool before filling.

These are favorites from my childhood which my mother makes.

Elaine Ewing, Sagaponack

Chocolate Potato Torte

1 cup butter
2 cups sugar
4 eggs, separated
½ cup cream or canned milk
1 cup freshly cooked, riced potatoes
1 cup chopped walnuts
4 ounces baking chocolate, melted
¼ teaspoon cloves
1 teaspoon cinnamon
1½ cups flour, sifted twice
1 teaspoon vanilla
Grated rind of one lemon
2 teaspoons baking powder

Cream butter and sugar; add egg yolks one at a time and beat. Add remaining ingredients except egg whites. Beat egg whites until stiff, and fold into mixture. Turn into nine-inch spring-form pan, and bake at 325 degrees for one and one-half hours. Cool. Decorate with chocolate frosting and a ring of halved maraschino cherries.

White Potato Torte

2 cups flour
2 teaspoons baking powder
1 teaspoon salt
¾ cup butter
1½ cups sugar
4 egg yolks
1 cup slightly warm riced potatoes
1 teaspoon vanilla
½ cup milk
1 cup chopped walnuts
4 egg whites
½ cup sugar

Sift flour with salt and baking powder. Cream butter and sugar gradually. Beat until light and fluffy. Add egg yolks one at a time and beat well after each. Blend in potatoes and vanilla. Alternate adding dry ingredients and milk to creamed mixture. Add nuts. Beat egg whites until they hold a peak, and gradually add one-half cup of sugar. Fold into cake mixture. Bake in 350 degree oven for one and one-quarter hours in 10-inch spring-form pan. Coat with a butter frosting when cooled.

Potato Flour Sponge Cake

This is a light cake which is acceptable for Passover use and is also good for diets requiring easily digestible foods.

7 egg yolks
2 whole eggs
1¾ cups confectioners sugar
2 teaspoons lemon juice
Rind of 1 lemon, grated
7 egg whites
1 scant cup sifted potato flour
⅛ teaspoon salt

Beat the egg yolks and whole eggs together. Add sugar gradually, and continue beating until thick and pale yellow. Add lemon juice and grated rind, beat thoroughly, add flour and salt and beat again. Beat egg whites until stiff but not dry, fold into yolk mixture and turn into a 10-inch tube pan. Bake 40 to 50 minutes in a 350 degree oven.

Potato Spice Cookies

Mrs. Clyde W. Cain, Flanders

1 cup molasses, heated
¾ cup shortening
1½ cups hot, riced potatoes
2 cups sifted flour
2 teaspoons baking powder
½ teaspoon baking soda
½ teaspoon salt
1 teaspoon cinnamon
½ teaspoon cloves
½ teaspoon nutmeg
½ cup raisins
2 tablespoons sugar (optional)

Heat molasses in a saucepan. Stir in shortening and remove from flame when melted. Add the hot potatoes and dry ingredients which have been sifted together. Add raisins and mix thoroughly. Drop by half-teaspoons upon waxed paper spread on baking sheets. Sprinkle with sugar if desired. Bake in moderately slow oven, 325 degrees, for 12 minutes or until firm and brown. Cool on a rack. Makes about 65 cookies.

Sweets

Potato Fluff Candy

Ethel Cosgrove, Sag Harbor

¾ cup mashed potatoes
1½ cups sugar
1 teaspoon lemon extract
1 cup cornflakes
1 cup chopped walnuts

Gradually work sugar into potatoes. Add remaining ingredients. Press into buttered pan, let stand 24 hours and cut into squares.

Potato Marzipan

¼ cup cold mashed potatoes
2 cups sifted confectioners sugar
8 ounces blanched almonds
1 egg white
1 tablespoon fresh lemon juice
½ teaspoon almond extract

Blend sugar and mashed potatoes. Pulverize almonds in an electric blender and add to potato-sugar mixture. Blend in remaining ingredients. Knead well with hands, adding a few drops of lemon juice if necessary. The dough may be divided into small batches and mixed with vegetable food colorings, or it may be shaped into flowers, fruits, animals or other figures first and then painted with food coloring diluted with water. Yields about one pound of candy.

Potato Crafts

Potato Printing

You will need potatoes, a sharp knife, some poster paint, ink or food coloring, and brown wrapping paper, newsprint, tissue or other kind of paper. Cut the potato in half. Either use the cut potato shape itself, or draw or stencil a simple design such as a star, heart, letter of the alphabet, et-cetera, and cut away the background to a depth of about one-quarter inch so that the design is in relief.

Pour some poster paint into a shallow dish. If you are using ink or food coloring, pour some onto a small piece of sponge, which will serve as a stamp pad and prevent dripping.

Carefully dip the cut-out edge of the potato into the paint or ink, and then stamp onto the paper. Repeat for an all over pattern.
The potato-printed paper may be used as book covers, gift wrapping, or to cover coffee cans for kitchen canisters, decorate tissue boxes or card-board boxes, and a variety of other uses.

Potato Valentine

Cut a potato in half and draw a heart, flower, tree or other simple design on one surface. Cut away a bit of potato around the design so that the design stands out in low relief, but be sure to leave the edges of the potato intact. Paint the cut surfaces of both halves of the potato with acrylic paint, inscribe message and allow to dry. Then put the halves of the potato together and tie with ribbon. The potato will dry up eventually and harden but the painted surfaces will remain brightly colored and readable forever. Or put a small gift in, such as a ring or other object.

Half a potato, pierced with an ice pick in several places and placed flat side down in a vase of water, makes a fine holder for flower stems.

Potato Puppets

If you can find potatoes with odd bumps and irregularities that suggest facial features, choose these, although any shape will do.
Using an apple corer or small knife, cut a hole in one end of the potato large enough for the index finger.

The face may be carved into the potato, or may be painted or pasted on with bits of wood, shells, buttons, pins, thumbtacks, etcetera. Scraps of yarn, cotton batting, string, steel wool, wood shavings or curled paper may be used for hair. An old mitten, sock or square of cloth with a hole in it for the index finger to go through makes a ready costume, and these may be stuffed for more body.

The puppets may also be manipulated on sticks instead of on the finger. This is particularly good for shadow shows if the puppets have clearly defined features.

The puppet stage can be simply a table, covered in front, or a doorway with a sheet or curtain stretched across the bottom half to conceal the puppeteer. An inexpensive tension rod for curtains may be found at the dime store which is an easy way of suspending the fabric.

A shadow stage can be constructed from a cardboard carton. Turn it open side down, and cut out the front and back panels, leaving a one-inch or two-inch border from each edge to prevent the box from collapsing. Then paste a rectangle of white sheet or tissue across the front. Light the stage brightly from the rear, and hold the puppets close to the screen so that their features are sharply delineated.

Who Says A Potato Has To Be Bald

Scoop out a bit of pulp from the top of a large potato and stuff in a little moistened cotton. Stick in some cloves for eyes, a snip of the potato top for a nose, and a sliver of carrot for a mouth. Slice off the bottom of the potato and set it in a small dish of water on the window sill. Sprinkle some grass or bird seed on the cotton and water daily. Soon green hair will sprout.

A slice of raw potato will clean wood and silver.

Potato Games

One Potato, Two Potato

This is a game of elimination. Players stand in a line or circle, fists in front of them, thumb and forefinger upward. The first player recites the following rhyme, lightly tapping each fist in succession, including his own. The player whose fist is tapped on the word "more" must put that hand behind his back.

> One potato, *two* potato
> *Three* potato, *four*
> *Five* potato, *six potato*
> *Seven* potato, *more.*

The rhyme is repeated in the same manner until only one fist remains, and that player is the winner.

Potato Sack Race

Each player is given a potato sack which he steps into and holds securely. At the signal "go," players must hop from the starting line to the finish line and back again. First one back wins.

Potato Race

Each player is given a basket or bowl which is placed at the starting line, about three feet apart. In front of each player are drawn four small circles, about four or five feet apart, depending upon how much space is available, each with a potato in it. At the signal "go", each player runs to the first circle, picks up the potato, and takes it back to the basket. Then he runs to the next circle, picks up the second potato and takes it back, and continues until all the potatoes are in the basket. The first one to finish wins. If there are several players, they may be divided into groups of twos, threes or fours, and the winners of each set can play each other for a final winner.

Potato Roll

Two circles are drawn in chalk on the floor or the sidewalk, each about four inches in diameter and about five feet apart. Players line up in teams, with the starting line for each eight feet from the circle. The first player on each team is given a table knife and a potato. He must place the potato on the starting line, and, at the signal "go", roll his potato with the knife across the floor and into the circle, and then back to the starting line. The next player then picks up the knife and potato and does the same. The first team to finish wins.

Hot Potato

Players sit in a circle and pass the potato clockwise from one to the next while someone outside the circle plays a musical instrument, a phonograph or radio. When the music stops, the player holding the potato is eliminated. This continues until there is a winner.

Steal The Tater

Players form two teams and line up facing each, 10 or 15 feet apart. Players are numbered consecutively on each team, beginning at opposite ends, so that number 1 faces number 10, number 2 faces number 9, and so forth. A potato is placed on the ground in the center between the two teams. A caller shouts out a number, and each of the two players with that number runs and tries to steal the potato and get back to his place without being tagged by the other one. If the player succeeds, his team earns one point. The game is over when one team earns the decided number of points for winning.

Potato Joust

Players are divided into pairs. Facing each other from a distance of three feet, each player must kneel on one knee and hold the other foot behind him with one hand. The other hand holds a fork with a potato securely impaled upon it. The objec is to knock the opponent's potato off his fork without losing one's own balance or potato. A player loses if his potato falls off the fork or if he falls three times. Pillows under the knees are permitted.

Look Ma No Hands

Players stand in a circle with their hands behind their backs. A large potato is placed under a player's chin, and then it is passed from one player's chin to the next, without the use of hands. A player is eliminated if he drops the potato or uses his hands.

Potato-Spoon Race

Players are divided into two teams and stand behind a starting line. An equal number of potatoes are placed in a row in front of each team. Eight feet from each team is a basket, and the first member of each team must pick up each potato with a teaspoon, using only one hand, and carry it to the basket. When all the potatoes are in the basket, he passes the spoon to the next member of the team who must reverse the procedure, returning the potatoes to the starting line, then passing the spoon to the next player. The first team to finish wins.

Bridge And Tunnel

Players line up in teams of equal number. The first player on each team is given a potato. At the signal, he must pass the potato over his head to the player behind him, who must pass it between his legs to the next player, who hands it over his head to the next, and so on to the last player, who then runs to the head of the line and passes it over his head to the player behind. The game continues until the first player is back in his original place. First team to finish wins.

What has eyes but cannot see?

Health and Beauty Lore

Hair Darkener

Dip a comb in water in which potatoes or potato parings have been boiled, and repeatedly comb through hair. Sunlight is believed to hasten the color and help set the dye.

Therapeutic Compress

Because potatoes retain heat or cold well, they are handy compresses. A cool potato applied to a vein is believed to reduce congestion.

Skin Whitener

Vegetable stains can be removed from the skin by rubbing them with a slice of raw potato.

Wrinkle Remover

Envelop a teaspoon of grated raw potato in a compress of surgical gauze. Place a compress over each eye (closed) for 15 minutes. This is said to smooth eyelid wrinkles.

Rheumatism Cure

A potato carried in a pocket or hung around the neck on a string and allowed to dry is an old-time cure and preventative for rheumatism.

Baked Potato and Buttermilk Diet

One baked potato daily, complete with skin, and six glasses of buttermilk spaced out during the day. I've known some very heavy individuals to stay on this diet for months. As should be done in every case, the blood and urine were checked particularly for any deficiencies. In practically every case I found the individuals in sound physical condition with health much improved by sizeable losses in weight.

From the book, *The Doctor's Quick Weight Loss Diet,* by Stillman and Baker. Copyright 1967 by Samm Sinclair Baker and Irwin Maxwell Stillman, M. D. Reprinted with permission of the publisher, Prentice-Hall, Inc., Englewood Cliffs, New Jersey

Potato Glossary

hot potato. A project or an idea for which no one wants to assume responsibility; something no one is willing to handle.

meat-and-potatoes man. A male person of basic, uncomplicated tastes.

Murphy. Synonym for potato, possibly derived from the name of a successful farmer, having been shortened from "Murphy's potatoes."

potato. 1. The head or face. 2. A dollar.

potato head. A stupid person.

potato jaw. A mouth.

potato nose. An unattractive nose.

potato trap. A mouth.

small potatoes. Insignificant; not amounting to much.

spud. A potato. One theory traces this term to an acronym from the "Society for the Prevention of an Unwholesome Diet," presumably a group which fought to keep the potato out of England. More likely the term originally meant a type of digging fork used in raising potatoes.

spuddy. A disreputable seller of bad potatoes.

tu me dices papas. Spanish expression meaning "you are telling me fibs," or literally "you are telling me potatoes."

Poème de Terre

I like them delicately boiled,
I like them French and quickly fried;
I like them baked and rissoléed,
They turn me on when shepherd-pied.

I like them souffléed, au gratin,
Adore them when they're mashed and buttery.
Chowders can't begin without them,
Knishes make my heart quite fluttery.

With corned beef hash they are a must,
They yodel in a Swiss raclette;
Shoestring, scalloped or O'Brien,
My appetite is *sans* regret.

How lovely is a Vichyssoise!
How cool Kartoffelen salad!
Oh, Lyonnaise and Dauphinoise,
You make my stomach really glad.

Solanum Tuberosum, hail!
Despite your warty, grotesque mien,
Despite your common-garden look,
We sing to you a noble paean.

Oh, face that launched a thousand chips,
To you, the fish and I do sing!
Oh, flesh that lunched a thousand chefs,
You're such an unassuming thing.

I pose this question now to all;
To gourmets, pundits, Freuds and Platos...
In any civilized cuisine,
What would we do..without..potatoes?

John W. Little II